Dixmude

FRENCH MARINES MARCHING OUT OF THEIR DEPOT AT
THE GRAND PALAIS, PARIS

Dixmude
French Marines in the
Great War, 1914-1918

Charles Le Goffic

LEONAUR

Dixmude: French Marines in the Great War, 1914-1918
by Charles Le Goffic

Leonaur is an imprint of Oakpast Ltd

Material original to this edition and presentation of the
text in this form copyright © 2011 Oakpast Ltd

ISBN: 978-0-85706-745-6 (hardcover)
ISBN: 978-0-85706-746-3 (softcover)

http://www.leonaur.com

Publisher's Note

Contents

Introduction

Praise, they say, is stricken dumb by the greatest names, and also, we may add, by the greatest deeds. It is only by the bare simplicity of faithful narrative that we can hope not to belittle these.

But yesterday the public had no knowledge of the great, heroic things accomplished by the Brigade of Marines (*Fusiliers Marins*). They were hidden under a confused mass of notes, *communiqués*, instructions and plans of operations, private letters, and newspaper articles. It has been no easy task to bring them to light—the discreet light permitted by the censorship. Everything seems simple and obvious to those who can look at facts in their logical order and regular sequence. The historian who has to handle new matter knows what a labour it is to introduce, or rather to re-establish, such order and sequence. History has to be written before the philosophy of history can be evolved.[1]

Our readers must not be surprised, therefore, to find here only such considerations as are in direct relation to events. We have been concerned with facts rather than with ideas. And in the result nothing will be lost hereby, for we provide materials ready for use in the establishment of that war mysticism which the sombre genius of Joseph de Maistre presaged, which Vigny showed at work in certain souls, and which is marked out as our national religion of tomorrow. It is obvious that such an immense effort, such prolonged tension, such whole-hearted sacrifice, as were demanded from the handful of men with whom we are concerned, could not have been obtained by ordinary methods. A special compact was

---

1. We may perhaps be allowed to note that Dixmude appeared in the *Revue des Deux Mondes*, March 1 and 15, before any other study on the subject.

required, a peculiar state of grace; the miracle was only possible as the outcome of a close communion, and, to use the proper word, of a true spiritual fraternity between men and officers.

True, this fraternity has been manifested in every branch of the service and on every battlefield during the course of the present struggle; but nowhere perhaps has it been so absolute as among the marines. They had, no doubt, been well prepared. The sea is a perpetual battlefield, and a trench is hardly more of a prison than a ship. Community of danger soon creates community of hearts; how otherwise can we account for the fact that the most turbulent and individualist of men become the most perfectly disciplined on board ship? This is the case with the Bretons. At Dixmude under the command of their own officers, retaining not only the costume, but the soul and the language of their profession, they were still sailors. Grouped with them were seamen from all our naval stations, Bayonne, Toulon, Dunkirk, etc., and the battalion of Commander de Sainte-Marie, formed at Cherbourg, even contained a fair sprinkling of natives of Les Batignolles. I had opportunities of talking to several of these "Parigots," and I should not advise anyone to speak slightingly of their officers before them, though, indeed, so few of these have survived that nine times out of ten the quip could be aimed only at a ghost. The deepest and tenderest words I heard uttered concerning Naval Lieutenant Martin des Pallières were spoken by a marine of the Rue des Martyrs, Georges Delaballe, who was one of his gunners in front of the cemetery the night when his machine-guns were jammed, and five hundred Germans, led by a major wearing the Red Cross armlet, threw themselves suddenly into our trenches.

"But why did you love him so?" I asked.

"I don't know.... We loved him because he was brave, and was always saying things that made us laugh, ... but above all because he loved us."

Here we have the secret of this extraordinary empire of the officers over their men, the explanation of that miracle of a four weeks' resistance, one against six, under the most formidable tempest of shells of every calibre that ever fell upon a position, in a shattered town where all the buildings were ablaze, and where, to quote the words of a *Daily Telegraph* correspondent, it was no longer light or dark, "but only red." When the Boches murdered Commander Jeanniot, his men were half crazy. They would not have felt the death of a father more deeply. I have recently had a letter sent me written by a Breton lad, Jules Cavan, who was wounded at Dixmude. While he was in hospital at Bordeaux he was visited by relatives of Second-Lieutenant Gautier, who was killed on October 27 in the cemetery trenches. The following day he wrote to M. Dalché de Desplanels:

Dear Sir,
You cannot imagine how your visit went to my heart.... On October 19, when my battalion took the offensive at Lannes, three kilometres from Dixmude, I was wounded by a bullet in the thigh. I dragged myself along as best I could on the battlefield, bullets falling thickly all around me. I got over about five hundred metres on the battlefield and reached the road. Just at that moment Lieutenant Gautier, who was coming towards me with a section, seeing me in the ditch, asked: 'Well, my lad, what is the matter with you?' 'Oh, lieutenant, I am wounded in the leg, and I cannot drag myself further.' 'Here then, get on my back.' And he carried me to a house at Lannes, and said these words, which I shall never forget: 'Stay there, my lad, till they come and fetch you. I will let the motor ambulance men know.' Then he went off under the fire. Oh, the splendid fellow!

"The splendid fellow!" Jules Cavan echoes Georges Delaballe, the Breton, the "Parigot." There is the same heartfelt ring in the words of each. And sometimes, as I muse over these heroic shades, I ask myself which were the more admirable, officers or men. When Second-Lieutenant Gautier received orders to take the place of Lieutenant de Pallières, buried by a shell in the trench of the cemetery where Lieutenant Eno had already fallen, he read his fate plainly; he said: "It's my turn." And he smiled at Death, who beckoned him. But I know of one case when, as Death seemed about to pass them by, the marines provoked it; when, after they had used up all their cartridges and were surrounded in a barn, twelve survivors only remaining with their captain, the latter, filled with pity for them, and recognising the futility of further resistance, said to his men: "My poor fellows, you have done your duty. There is nothing for it but to surrender."

Then, disobedient to their captain for the first time, they answered: "No!"

To my mind nothing could show more clearly the degree of sublime exaltation and complete self-forgetfulness to which our officers had raised the morale of their men. Such were the pupils these masters in heroism had formed, that often their own pupils surpassed them. There was at the Trouville Hospital a young Breton sailor called Michel Folgoas. His wound was one of the most frightful imaginable: the whole of his side was shaved off by a shell which killed one of his comrades in the trenches, who was standing next to him, on November 2. He remarks in a letter:

> I was completely stunned at first. When I came to myself I walked three hundred metres before I noticed that I was wounded, and this was only when my comrades called out: '*Mon Dieu*, they have carried away half your side.'

It was true. But does he groans and lament over it? He makes a joke of it:

> The Boches were so hungry that they took a beef-steak out of my side, but this won't matter, as they have left me a little.

Multiply this Michel Folgoas by 6,000, and you will have the brigade. This inferno of Dixmude was an inferno where everyone made the best of things. And the *battues* of rabbits, the coursing of the red German hares which were running in front of the army of invasion, the bull-fights in which our Mokos impaled some pacific Flemish bull abandoned by its owners; more dubious escapades, sternly repressed, in the underground premises of the Dixmude drink-shops; a story of two Bretons who went off on a foraging expedition and were seen coming back along the canal in broad daylight towing a great cask of strong beer which they had unearthed Heaven knows where at a time when the whole brigade, officers as well as men, had nothing to drink but the brackish water of the Yser—these, and a hundred other tales of the same kind, which will some day delight village audiences gathered round festal evening fires, bear witness that Jean Gouin (or Le Gwenn, John the White, as the sailors call themselves familiarly[2]), did not lose his bearings even in his worst vicissitudes.

Dixmude was an epic then, or, as M. Victor Giraud proposes, a French *geste*, but a *geste* in which the heroism is entirely without solemnity or deliberation, where the nature of the seaman asserts itself at every turn, where there are thunder, lightning, rain, mud, cold, bullets, shrapnel, high explosive shells, and all the youthful gaiety of the French race. And this epic did not come to an end at Dixmude. The brigade did not ground arms after November 10. The gaps in its ranks being filled from the depots, it was kept up to the strength of two regiments, and reaped fresh laurels. At Ypres and Saint Georges it charged the troops of Prince Ruprecht of Bavaria and the Duke of Würtemberg in succession. Dixmude was but one panel of the triptych: on the broken apex of the black capital of the Communiers, on the livid backgrounds of the flat country about Nieuport, twice again did the brigade inscribe its stormy silhouette.

But at Ypres and Saint Georges the sailors had the bulk of the Anglo-French forces behind them; at Dixmude up to November 4 they knew that their enterprise was a forlorn hope. And in their hands they held the fate of the two Flanders. One of the heroes of Dixmude, Naval Lieutenant Georges Hébert, said that the Fusiliers had gained more than a naval battle there. My only objection to this statement is its modesty. Dixmude was our Thermopylae in the north, as the Grand-Couronné, near Nancy, was our Thermopylæ in the east; the Fusiliers were the first and the most solid element of the long triumphant defensive which will one day be known as the victory of the Yser, a victory less decisive and perhaps less brilliant than that of the Marne, but not less momentous in its consequences.

The *generalissimo* is credited with a dictum which he may himself have uttered with a certain astonishment:

"You are my best infantrymen," said he to the Fusiliers.

We will close with these simple, soldierly words, more eloquent than the most brilliant harangues. The brigade will reckon them among their proudest trophies to all time.

---

2. "When we passed through the streets of Ghent they were full of people shouting, 'Long live the French!' I heard one person in the crowd call out, 'Long live Jean Gouin!' He must have known them well." (Letter of Fusilier F., of the island of Sein.) Le Gwenn, which has been corrupted into Gouin, is a very common name in Brittany.

Note

The sources drawn upon in the following narrative are of various kinds: official *communiqués*, French and foreign reports, etc. But the majority of our information was derived from private letters, collected by M. de Thézac, the modest and zealous founder of the *Abris du Marin* (Seamen's Shelters), from note-books kindly lent by their owners, and from oral inquiries addressed to the survivors of Melle and Dixmude. Whenever possible, we have let our correspondents speak for themselves. We regret that the strictest orders have compelled us to preserve their anonymity, which, however, we hope may be merely temporary.

CHAPTER 1

Towards Ghent

On the morning of October 8 two troop trains passed each other in the station of Thourout. One contained Belgian Carabiniers; the other, French marines. They exchanged greetings from their respective lines. The Carabiniers waved their little yellow-bound caps and cried: "Long live France!" The sailors replied by hurrahs in honour of Belgium.

"Where are you going?" asked a Belgian officer.

"To Antwerp. And you?"

"To France."

He explained that the Carabiniers were recruits from La Campine, who were being sent to our lines to finish their training.

"You'll soon get them into shape, won't you?" said a sailor to the officer. And shaking his fist at the horizon, he added:

"Don't you worry, lieutenant! We shall get at the scum some day, never fear."

The Belgian officer who describes the scene, M. Edouard de Kayser,[1] had left Antwerp during the night. He did not know that the defence was at its last gasp, and that the evacuation had begun. Our sailors were no better informed. Rear-Admiral Ronarc'h, who was in command, thought that he was taking his brigade to Dunkirk; he had been given a week to form it and organise it on the footing of two regiments (six battalions and a machine-gun company). Everything had to be evolved: the complement of offic-

---

1. *Revue Hebdomadaire* of January 9, 1915. These were the same recruits which the last trains of marines passed in Dunkirk station. "October 8, 4 p.m. Arrived at Dunkirk. Passed the Belgian class 1914. Many cries of 'Long live France!'" (Second-Lieutenant Gautier's pocket-book. See also p. 5, n.).

15

ers, the men, the auxiliary services. This arduous task was complicated by the lack of cohesion among the elements of the brigade and perpetual changes of quarters (Creil, Stains, Pierrefitte, etc.). But the idea of forming infantry brigades with sailors was an afterthought. Article 11 of the Law of August 8, 1913, certainly permitted any surplus men in the navy to be used for service in the field, but the manner in which these contingents were to be employed had never been clearly defined. Would they be linked to existing bodies, or would they be formed into separate units? The latter alternative, by far the most reasonable, which effected a gradual transition, and, while connecting the naval combatant with the land forces, preserved his somewhat jealous but very stimulating *esprit de corps*, was by no means unanimously approved. The Minister overruled objections, and he was well advised. The glorious lessons of 1870, of Le Bourget and Le Mans, had taught him what to expect from the co-operation of navy and army. Some preparation was of course necessary. Strictly speaking, a navy is made to navigate, and this explains a certain neglect of drill; these men in new clothes, "*capelés*" (cloaked), as they say, in the new fashion, their caps bereft of pompoms,[2] their collarless tunics buttoned up to the throat, had be transformed into soldiers. Handy as sailors proverbially are, a certain stiffness of movement in the early days betrayed the inexperience of these sea-birds, whose wings had been clipped; they were further hampered by heavy infantry overcoats. The brigade was sent almost immediately to the entrenched camp of Paris.[3] Scarcely had it settled into its quarters when its commander received orders to be ready to start for Dunkirk, where a new army was being formed. Dunkirk was not yet threatened; the brigade would be able to complete its organisation there. The order was dated October 4. On the morning of the 7th the brigade entrained at Saint Denis and at Villetaneuse with its convoys.

---

2. The pompons were restored after a time; at first they were considered too conspicuous; but regrettable mistakes had been made, and in the distance the headgear of our men was too much like the German caps.

3. A certain number of the men were there already. "For weeks we bivouacked in the entrenched camp of Paris, marching and countermarching to accustom the men to the novel weight of the knapsack. We spent the glorious days of the Marne as second line reserves and saw nothing." (Interview with Naval Lieutenant G. Hébert, by R. Kimley, *Opinion*, December 19, 1914.)

THE FLAG OF THE BRIGADE

"We are comfortably installed in cattle-trucks," notes Fusilier R. in his pocket-book. "At Creil we see houses that were burnt by the Germans. Night comes; we try to sleep, but in vain. It is very cold. We shiver in our trucks." But over the dunes, along which the train had been running since it left Boulogne, a patch of purple light appeared; then other fires twinkled, green and red, and the keen breath of the open sea made itself felt—Dunkirk. Here a surprise awaited the brigade: a change in the orders; it was not to turn out, but the trains were to go on "towards Belgium, towards the enemy," to Antwerp, in short.

The men stamped with joy. They hung over the doors of the trucks, waving their caps in greeting to Belgian territory.[4] The admiral went off in the first train with his staff. On the afternoon of the 8th he found General Pau on the platform at Ghent. The great organiser of the connections between the Allied Armies had just left Antwerp, where he had been to plan out the retreat of the Belgian army with King Albert. He informed the admiral that the railway had been cut above the town, and that the six divisions which were defending Antwerp had begun to fall back upon Bruges; two divisions were echeloned to the west of the Terneusen Canal, and three to the east. Only one division was still in Antwerp, with 10,000 English troops.[5] The Belgian cavalry was covering the retreat on the Scheldt, to the south of Lokeren. There was no longer any question of entering Antwerp; the contingent was to co-operate in the retreating movement with the English reinforcements which were expected, and with the troops of the garrison at Ghent; everything seemed to indicate that the enemy would try to gain ground in the west, and to invest the Belgian army, exhausted by two months of incessant fighting, and the forces from Antwerp that were supporting it at intervals along the Dutch frontier. But,

4. "At every station the inhabitants were massed on the platforms. Loud cheers were raised, and our compartments were literally filled with fruit, sandwiches, cigars, cigarettes, etc. Beer, tea, and coffee flowed freely. You can picture the delight of our marines, who imagined themselves in the Land of Promise." (Note-book of Dr. L. F.)
5. A Royal Naval Brigade and 6,000 volunteers from the Naval Reserve. These forces had only been in Antwerp, where they were preceded by Mr. Winston Churchill, since October 4. They fought very gallantly during the last days of the siege and gave most valuable support to the Belgian troops. In the course of the retreat which they helped to secure, a portion of them only was pressed back into Dutch territory and there interned.

to ensure the success of this enveloping manoeuvre, the Germans would first be obliged to take Ghent and Bruges, which they might so easily have done a month earlier; they had deliberately neglected this precaution, feeling confident that they would be able to occupy them at their own time without firing a shot.

By the end of August, indeed, General von Boehn's Army Corps had advanced to Melle, within a few miles of Ghent. Although no resistance had been offered, Melle had been partially burnt and pillaged; the Germans had spared only the distillery where their troops were quartered, which belonged to a naturalised Bavarian. To save the town from effective occupation by the enemy, the Burgomaster, M. Braun, had agreed with General von Boehn to undertake the victualling of the German troops stationed at Beleghem. The requisition was not a very harsh one for war time. But the foes were to meet again; on August 25, the morrow of Charleroi, the Kaiser would have cashiered a general as duly convicted of imbecility who had ventured to suggest that in October France, supposing her to be still alive, would have had strength enough in her death-throes to detach units and send them to the help of Belgium. Be this as it may, it is certain that the Belgian army owed its salvation to this erroneous calculation, or foolish presumption.

The effort the enemy had scorned to make in August against Ghent and West Flanders was now determined upon in October, after the fall of Antwerp. The conditions seemed to have changed but little. Ghent, an open town, spread over an alluvial plain at the confluence of the Scheldt and the Lys, which branch off here into innumerable canals, is open on every side to sudden assault. It has neither forts nor ramparts. We could only rely upon improvised defences to check the advance of the enemy. The garrison, under the command of General Clothen, was reduced to eight squadrons of cavalry, a mixed brigade, a volunteer brigade, and two line regiments, none of them up to full strength. However, with our 6,000 rifles, they would suffice to deploy in the loop of the Scheldt, and on the space between the Scheldt and the Lys to the south of the town, which seemed to be specially threatened. If the English 7th Division arrived in time on the following day, it would reinforce the front, which it would be unnecessary to extend further for the purposes of a purely temporary defence, designed to give the army in Antwerp an additional day or two. The fighting would probably be very severe; neither General Pau, who was responsible for the plan, nor Admiral Ronarc'h, who was to direct the principal effort, had any illusions on this score.

"Salute these gentlemen," said the general to his staff, pointing to the naval officers; "you will not see them again."[6]

The rest of the brigade followed hard upon the admiral. The last trains arrived at Ghent during the night. The whole population was astir, cheering the sailors as they marched through the town to their respective barracks: the Léopold Barracks, the Circus, and the Théâtre Flamand. The officers and the admiral were lodged at the Hôtel des Postes.[7] The reveillé was sounded at 4.30 a.m. The men drank their coffee and set off for Melle, where the Belgians had prepared trenches for them.

---

6. Cf. Jean Claudius, "*La Brigade Navale.*" (*Petite Gironae* of February 1, 1915.)

7. "I shared a room with the naval Lieutenant Martin des Pallières, and before going to bed we refreshed ourselves by a general toilet, our last ablutions during our stay in Belgium, and the last of all for my poor companion, who was killed at Dixmude." (Note-book of Dr. L. F.)

CHAPTER 2

The Battle of Melle

The little lace-making town, the younger sister of Mechlin and Bruges, had not suffered as much as we had feared. The rattle of the bobbins was no longer to be heard on the doorsteps; certain houses showed the stigmata of preliminary martyrdom in their empty window-frames and blackened façades. But her heart beat still, and around her, in the great open conservatory which forms the outskirts of Ghent, Autumn had gathered all her floral splendours. "We marched through fields of magnificent begonias, among which we are perhaps about to die," wrote Fusilier R. To die among flowers like a young girl seems a strange destiny for the conventional sailor—the typical sea-dog with a face tanned by sun and spray. But the majority of the recruits of the brigade bore little resemblance to the type. Their clear eyes looked out of faces but slightly sunburnt; the famous "Marie-Louises" were hardly younger.[1] Their swaying walk and a touch of femininity and coquetry in the precocious development of their muscular vigour explain the nickname given them by the heavy Teutons, to whom they were as disconcerting as an apparition of boyish Walkyries: *the young ladies with the red pompoms!* The admiral, who had just reconnoitred the position, was conferring with his lieutenants on the spot; a fraction of the 2nd Regiment, under Commander Varney, was to take up a position between Gontrode and Quatrecht, leaving a battalion in reserve to the north of Melle; a fraction of the 1st Regiment, under Commander Delage, was to advance between Heusden and Goudenhaut, and to leave a battalion in reserve at Destelbergen. He himself would keep

---

1. Napoleon's young recruits of 1813, who called themselves after the Empress.

21

with him as general reserve, at the cross-roads of Schelde, which was to be his post of command, the rest of the brigade, that is to say, two battalions and the machine-gun company.

The convoys, with the exception of the ambulances commanded by Staff-Surgeon Seguin, were to stay in the rear, at the gates of Ghent. This was an indispensable precaution in view of a rapid retreat, which, however, the admiral had no intention of carrying out until he had sufficiently broken the shock of the enemy's onslaught.

Thanks to our reinforcements, the Belgian troops were able to extend their front as much as was necessary by occupying Lemberge and Schellerode. The artillery of the 4th mixed Brigade, emplaced near Lendenhock, commanded the approaches of the plain. No trace of the enemy was to be seen. But the Belgian cyclist scouts had brought in word that the German vanguard had crossed the Dendre. We had only just time to occupy our trenches; in the last resort, if it should be necessary to fall back on Melle, we should find a ready-made epaulement in the railway embankment near the station bridge.

Antwerp was burning, and the civic authorities were parleying over its surrender; the English forces and the last Belgian division had fortunately been able to leave the town during the night; they blew up the bridges behind them, and made for Saint Nicolas by forced marches, arriving there at dawn. They hoped to reach Eeclo by evening. But the enemy was hard in pursuit; a party of German cavalry was sighted at Zele and near Wetteren, where they crossed the Scheldt on a bridge of boats. At the village of Basteloere they fell in with the Belgian outposts, whose artillery stopped them for the time; other forces, further to the north, advanced in the district of Waïs as far as Loochristi, 10 kilometres from Ghent. Part of these came from Alost, the rest from Antwerp itself; but the bulk of the German troops remained at Antwerp, to our great satisfaction.

An enemy less arrogant or less bent on theatrical effect would undoubtedly have thrown his whole available forces on the rear of the retreat; the Germans preferred to make a sensational entry into Antwerp, with fifes sounding and ensigns spread.[2]

---

2. As a matter of fact, this triumphal entry, followed by a review of the investing army with massed bands, did not take place till the afternoon of the following Sunday. But the criticism holds good: only a portion of the German forces went in pursuit of the Belgian army after repairing the bridge across the Scheldt; 60,000 men remained in Antwerp.

Simultaneously, the troops they had detached at Alost had their first encounter with the 2nd Regiment of the Brigade. They were expected, and a few well-directed volleys sufficed to check their ardour. To quote one of our Fusiliers, "they fell like ninepins" at each discharge. "There was plenty of whistling round our heads, too," writes another of the combatants, who expresses his regret at having been unable "to grease his bayonet in the bellies of the Germans." He had his chance later. The enemy returned in force, and Commander Varney thought it advisable to call up his reserve, which was at once replaced at Melle by a battalion of the general reserve. "There was," says Dr. Caradec, "a certain gun which was run up by the Germans about 800 metres from the trenches; it had only just fired its fourth shot when we blew up its team and its gunners. They were not able to get it away till nightfall." Indeed, generally speaking, the enemy's fire, which was too long in range, did very little damage to us in the course of this battle; the town did not suffer appreciably, and only three shells struck the church. Towards six o'clock the attack ceased. Night was falling; a slight mist floated over the fields, and the enemy took advantage of it to solidify his position. Pretending to retire, he remained close at hand, occupying the woods, the houses, the hedges, the farmyards, and every obstacle on the ground. These were unequivocal signs of a speedy resumption of the offensive. Commander Varney, whose contingents bore the brunt of the pressure, was not deceived and kept a sharp look-out. The men were forbidden to stir; they were told that they must eat when they could. Besides, they had nothing for a meal. "It was not until midnight," says Fusilier R., "that I was able to get a little bread; I offered some of it to my Commander, who accepted it thankfully." The mist lifted, but it was still very dark. Black night on every hand, save down by Quatrecht, where two torches were blazing, two farms that had been fired. The men listened, straining their ears. It was just a watch, on land instead of at sea. But nothing stirred till 9 o'clock. Then suddenly the veil was rent: shells with luminous fuses burst a few yards from the trenches; the enemy had received artillery reinforcements; our position was soon to become untenable. "We saw the Boches by the light of the shells, creeping along the hedges and houses like rats. We fired into the mass, and brought them down in heaps, but they kept on advancing. The Commander was unwilling for us to expose ourselves further; he gave orders to abandon Gontrode and fall back a little further upon Melle, behind the railway bank."[3]

We lost a few men in the retreat. But our position was excellent. About 60 metres from the trenches our machine-guns poured out hell-fire on the enemy, whom we had allowed to approach. A splendid charge by the Fusiliers completed his discomfiture. It was four in the morning. At 7 a.m. our patrols brought us word that Gontrode and Quatrecht were evacuated; the Germans had not even stopped to pick up their wounded.

The Fusiliers did this good office for them when they went to reoccupy Gontrode, taking the opportunity to collect a good number of German helmets.[4] Meanwhile the brigade had passed under the command of General Capper, of the 7th English Division, who had just arrived at Ghent, where his men received an ovation like that bestowed on our own sailors. Indeed, there is a strong likeness between them. The Englishmen in their dark dun-coloured uniform, with their clear eyes and rhythmic gait, are also of an ocean race, and do not forget it. They swung along, their rifles under their arms, or held by the barrel against their shoulders like oars, singing the popular air adopted by the whole British army: *It's a long, long way to Tipperary.*

Apparently Ghent lies on the road to this goal, for the *Tommies* can never have been gayer. These fine troops, which advanced to the firing line as if they had been going to a Thames regatta, were the admiration not only of the citizens of Ghent, but of our own sailors, who felt an unexpected tenderness for them. Had not the hereditary foe become our staunchest ally?

---

3. Fusilier Y. M. J., *Correspondence*. See also the letter of the sailor P. L. Y., of Audierne; "Then, seeing that they were advancing against us in mass (they were a regiment against our single company), we were obliged to fall back 400 metres, for we could no longer hold them. I saw the master-at-arms fall mortally wounded, and four men wounded when we got back to the railway line. There we stayed for a day and a night to keep the Boches employed, sending volleys into them when they came too near and charging them with the bayonet. It was fine to see them falling on the plain at every volley. We ceased firing on the 10th, about 4 a.m."

4. "This morning we made a fine collection of dead Germans from 50 to 100 metres from our trenches. We have a few prisoners." (Letter from Second-Lieutenant Gautier.)

"We look upon them as brothers," wrote a sailor of the Passage Lauriec to his family next day.

Reinforced by two of their battalions and the Belgian troops of the sector, we were ordered to hold our former positions in the loop of the Scheldt. But towards noon, after a visit from a Taube, the enemy developed such a fierce attack upon Gontrode and Quatrecht that at the end of the day we had to repeat the manoeuvre of the preceding day and fall back upon the railway bank. Here at least the German offensive spent itself in vain upon the glacis of this natural redoubt, defended with conspicuous gallantry by Commander Varney's three battalions. The rest of the night was quiet; the reliefs came into the trenches normally at dawn, and those who wished were free to go to church. It was a Sunday. "I have been to mass in a very pretty little church," wrote Seaman F., of the Isle of Sein. The day passed very well. In the evening after supper we went to bed. Scarcely had we lain down upon the straw when the order was given to turn out again.

We were to beat a retreat, and it was time. The apparent inactivity of the enemy during this day of the 11th of October was explained by his desire to turn our position and surround us with all his forces in the loop of the Scheldt. On both banks of the river, down-stream and to the south, long grey lines were writhing. It was a question whether it would be wise to expose ourselves further, and to give the enemy a pretext for bombarding Ghent, an open town, which we had decided not to defend. Had we not achieved our main object, since our resistance of the previous days had given the Belgian army forty-eight hours' start? Headquarters acknowledged that we had carried out our mission unfalteringly. From the moment when they first came into touch with the enemy the Naval Fusiliers had behaved with the firmness and endurance of tried troops, like "old growlers," as Fusilier R. said. Twice the German infantry had given way to their irresistible charge. This gave good hope for the future.

Our own casualties had been inconsiderable. Ten of our men had been killed, among them Naval Lieutenant Le Douget, who had been in the trenches, with his company, and who had been mortally wounded by a bullet as he was falling back on the railway embankment; we had 39 wounded and one missing, whereas, according to the official *communiqué*, the enemy's losses were 200 killed and 50 prisoners.[5]

Melle was not a great battle, but it was a victory, "our first victory," said the men proudly, the first canto of their Iliad. And the troops which gained this victory were under fire for the first time. They came from the five ports, mainly from Brittany, which provides four-fifths of the combatants for naval warfare. And the majority of them, setting aside a few warrant-officers, were young apprentices taken from the depots before they had finished their training, but well stiffened by non-commissioned officers of the active list and the reserve. The officers themselves, with the exception of the commanders of the two regiments (Captains Delage and Varney), who ranked as colonels, and the battalion commanders (Captains Rabot, Marcotte de Sainte-Marie, and De Kerros, 1st Regiment; Jeanniot, Pugliesi-Conti, and Mauros, 2nd Regiment), belonged for the most part to the Naval Reserve. It was, in fact, a singular army, composed almost entirely of recruits and veterans, callow youths and greybeards. There were even some novices of the Society of Jesus, Father de Blic and Father Poisson,[6] serving as sub-lieutenants, and a former Radical deputy, Dr. Plouzané,[7] who acted as surgeon. The percentage of casualties was very high among the older men at the beginning of the campaign, and this has been

---

5. According to *Le Temps* of October 18, the German losses were very much greater: "800 Germans killed." The hesitation and want of vigour shown in the attack seem surprising. They are perhaps to be explained by the following passage, written by Second-Lieutenant de Blois: "The Germans had not expected such a resistance, and even less had they thought to find us in front of them. They suspected a trap, and this paralysed their offensive, though our line was so thin that a vigorous onslaught could not have failed to break it. This they did not dare to make; several times they advanced to within a few metres of our trenches and then stopped short. We shot them down at our ease. Yet our positions were far from solid; we were on the railway embankment, and the trenches consisted of a few holes dug between the rails; the bridge had not even been barricaded by the Belgian engineers, and nothing would have been simpler than to have passed under it. When night came, Commander Conti ordered me to see to it. I turned on a little electric pocket light; the bullets at once began to whistle about my ears; the Germans were only about 20 metres from the bridge, but they made no attempt to pass!"

6. The first killed and the second wounded at Dixmude. Both received the Legion of Honour.

7. He also received the Legion of Honour.

26

made a reproach to them. If a great many officers fell, it was not due to bravado, still less to ignorance of the profession of arms, as has been suggested[8]; but leaders must preach by example, and there is only one way of teaching others to die bravely. We must not forget that their men were recruits, without homogeneity, without experience, almost without training. The morale of troops depends on that of their chiefs. "If you go about speaking to no one, sad and pensive," said Monluc, "even if all your men had the hearts of lions, you would turn them into sheep." This was certainly the opinion of the officers of the brigade, and notably of him who commanded the 2nd Regiment, Captain Varney, "always in the breach," according to an eye-witness, "going on foot to the first lines and the out-posts and even beyond them, as at Melle. Here," adds the narrator, "he was on an armoured car, but ... on the step, entirely without cover, to give confidence to his men." One of the officers of his regiment, Lieutenant Gouin,[9] wounded in the foot in the same en-counter, refused to go to the ambulance until the enemy began to retreat; Second-Lieutenant Gautier,[10] commanding a machine-gun section, allowed a German attack to advance to within 60 metres, "to teach the gunners not to squander their ammunition," and when wounded in the head, said: "What does it matter, since every one of my 502 bullets found its billet?"

Moreover, the chief of these gallant fellows, Rear-Admiral Ronarc'h, had proved himself a strategist on other battle-fields; the Minister's choice was due neither to complaisance nor to chance.

Admiral Ronarc'h is a Breton; his guttural, sonorous name is almost a birth-certificate. And physically the man answers exactly to the image evoked by his name and race. His short, sturdy, broad-shouldered figure is crowned by a rugged, resolute head, the planes strongly marked, but refined, and even slightly ironical; he has the true Celtic eyes, slightly veiled, which seem always to be looking at things afar off or within; morally he is, as one of his officers says:

> ... a furze-bush of the cliffs, one of those plants that flour-ish in rough winds and poor soil, that strike root among the

---

8. Cf. Dr. Caradec, "*La Brigade des Fusiliers Marins de l'Yser*" (*Dépêche de Brest* for January 19, 1915).
9. Killed at Dixmude.
10. Killed at Dixmude.

crevices of granite rocks and can never be detached from them: Breton obstinacy in all its strength, but a calm, reflective obstinacy, very sober in its outward manifestations, and concentrating all the resources of a mind very apt in turning the most unpromising elements to account upon its object.[11]

It is rather remarkable that all the great leaders in this war are taciturn and thoughtful men; never has the antithesis of deeds and words been more strongly marked. It has been noted elsewhere that Admiral Ronarc'h, though a very distinguished sailor,[12] seems destined to fight mainly as a soldier in war; as a naval lieutenant and adjutant-major to Commander de Marolles, he accompanied the Seymour column sent to the relief of the European Legations when the Boxers besieged them in Pekin. The column, which was too weak, though it was composed of sailors of the four European naval divisions stationed in Chinese waters, was obliged to fall back hurriedly towards the coast. It was almost a defeat, in the course of which the detachments of the Allied divisions lost a great many men and all the artillery they had landed. The French detachment was the only one which brought off its guns. The author of this fine strategic manoeuvre was rewarded by promotion to the command of a frigate; he was then 37 years old. At the date of his promotion (March 23, 1902) he was the youngest officer of his rank. At 49, in spite of his grizzled moustache and "imperial," he is the youngest of our admirals. He attained his present rank in June, 1914, and was almost immediately called upon to form the Marine Brigade.

---

11. Dr. L. G., private correspondence.
12. He won his stars as commander of the Mediterranean Fleet, and has invented a mine-sweeper adopted by the British navy.

CHAPTER 3

Retreat

How was the retirement to be carried out?

The operation seemed to be a very delicate one. The enemy was watching us on every side. General Capper's orders were to disengage ourselves by a night march to Aeltre, where the roads to Bruges and Thielt intersect. The retreat began very accurately and methodically, facilitated by the precautionary arrangements the admiral had made: first, our convoys; then, half an hour later, our troops, which were replaced temporarily in their positions by the English units. "As we passed through Ghent," writes Fusilier B., "we were heartily cheered again, the more so as some of us had taken Prussian helmets, which they showed to the crowd. The enthusiasm was indescribable. The ladies especially welcomed us warmly." Fair Belgium had given us her heart; she did not withdraw it, even when we seemed to be forsaking her. Covered by the English division which followed us after the space of two hours, we passed through Tronchiennes, Luchteren, Meerendré, Hansbeke, and Bellem, a long stretch of eight leagues, by icy moonlight, with halts of ten minutes at each stage. The motor-cars of the brigade rolled along empty, all the officers, even the oldest of them, electing to march with their men. Aeltre was not reached till dawn. The brigade had not been molested in its retreat; we lost nothing on the way, neither a straggler nor a cartridge. And all our dead, piously buried the night before by the chaplain of the 2nd Regiment, the Abbé Le Helloco, with the help of the *curé* and the Burgomaster, were sleeping in the little churchyard of Melle.

After snatching a hasty meal and resting their legs for a while, the men started for Thielt. "Twenty-five kilometres on top of the forty we had done in the night," says a Fusilier, somewhat hyperbolically. "And they say sailors are not good walkers!"[1]

To avoid corns, they marched bare-footed, their boots slung over their shoulders. And they had to drag the machine-guns, for which there were no teams. But Aeltre, the kindness of its inhabitants, the good coffee served out, and laced by a generous municipal ration of rum, had revived them. "What good creatures they are!" said a Fusilier. "They receive us as if we were their own children!"

The brigade reached Thielt between four and five in the afternoon; the English division arrived at six, and we at once went into our temporary quarters; the roads were barricaded, and strong guards were placed at every issue. Fifty thousand Germans were galloping in pursuit of us. If they did not catch us at Thielt, we perhaps owed this to the Burgomaster of one of the places we had passed through, who sent them on a wrong track. His heroic falsehood cost him his life, and secured a good night's rest for our men. For the first time for three days they were able to sleep their fill on the straw of hospitable Belgian farms and make up for the fatigues of their previous vigils. A Taube paid an unwelcome visit in the morning, but was received with a vigorous fusillade, and the "beastly bird" was brought down almost immediately, falling in the English lines, to the great delight of our men. Shortly afterwards we broke up our camp and set out for Thourout, which we reached at 1 p.m. Here the English di-

---

1. This was one of the first questions General Pau put to the admiral: "Are your men good walkers?" He foresaw that they might have to execute a very rapid retreat. Our officers felt some anxiety on this score. "When not in danger," says Dr. L. F. in his note-book, "the sailor gets rusty. At the beginning of October all of us, officers and men alike, had received the blue infantry overcoat, which was obligatory. The men shouldered knapsacks (not without grumbling), and we were transformed into troopers, nothing left of naval uniform but our caps.... This part of the foot-soldier assigned to them seems an inferior one to our men, and they accept it unwillingly, especially when it entails military marches with great-coats and haversacks. We had innumerable limpers and laggards on our marches in the environs of Paris. The contrast was very striking to those who saw our men afterwards in Belgium. It was a proof of the marvellous resilience of our race, and more particularly of our Bretons, who are always in the majority in the brigade."

vision had to leave us, to march upon Roulers, and the brigade came under the command of King Albert, whose outposts we had now reached.

The Belgian army, after its admirable retreat from Antwerp, had merely touched at Bruges, and deciding not to defend Ostend, had fallen back by short marches towards the Yser. All its convoys had not yet arrived. To ensure their safety, it had decided, in spite of its exhausted state, to deploy in an undulating line extending from Menin to the marshes of Ghistelles; the portion of this front assigned to the Fusiliers ran from the wood of Vijnendaele to the railway station of Cortemarck. On the 14th, in a downpour of rain, the brigade marched to the west of Pereboom, and took up a position facing east. It was the best position open to them, though, indeed, it was poor enough, by reason of its eccentricity. The enemy, who had finally got on our track, was reported to be advancing in dense masses upon Cortemarck. The 6,000 men of the brigade, however heroic they might prove themselves, could not hope to offer a very long resistance to such overwhelming forces on a position so difficult to maintain, a position without natural defences, without cover on any side, even towards the west, where the French troops had not yet completed their extension. It was the admiral's duty to report to the Belgian headquarters staff on these tactical defects; the reply was an order to make a stand "at all costs," a term fully applicable to the situation; but this was rescinded, and at midnight on October 15 the retreat was resumed.

It ceased only on the banks of the Yser.

CHAPTER 4

On the Yser

Our columns started at 4 a.m., while it was still quite dark, but the roads were good in spite of the rain which had been falling incessantly all night.

The route was through Warken, Zarren, and Eessen, with Dixmude as its final point. The first battalion of the 2nd Regiment and the three Belgian batteries of the Pontus group brought up the rear. The advance was hampered by the usual congestion of the roads, refugees fleeing before the invaders, dragging bundles containing all their worldly goods. These miserable beings seemed to be moving along mechanically, their legs the only part of them that showed any vitality. They halted by the roadside, making way for us, staring at us dully, as if they had left their souls behind them with all the dear familiar things of their past lives. Our men called out to them as they passed: "Keep your hearts up. We'll come back."

They made no answer. It was still raining, and the water was streaming off the great-coats. Near Eessen we left Commander de Kerros with the second battalion of the 1st Regiment, to hold the roads of Vladsloo, Clercken, and Roulers; the third battalion of the 2nd Regiment, under Commander Mauros, pushed on in the direction of Woumen, to bar the way to Ypres. We had a fine front, though the admiral thought it rather too wide for our strength. The four other battalions and the machine-gun company entered Dixmude about noon, and at once took up a position behind the Yser after detaching a strong outpost guard on the north, near the village of Beerst, on the Ostend road, by the side of which runs a little light railway for local transport. The admi-

La Grand Place, Dixmude

ral, who had been anxiously looking out for some undulation in this desperately flat landscape where he could place his artillery, found a suitable spot at last to the south of the Chapel of Notre Dame de Bon Secours, half-way to Eessen. He chose the chapel itself for his own headquarters. All these arrangements were made immediately, and the men had scarcely got into their quarters, when they were sent out with spades and picks, together with a company of the Belgian Engineers, to put the outskirts of the town into a state of defence. They had to be content with measures of the greatest urgency alone, for the enemy was pressing in upon us and creeping up to Dixmude. A few shrapnel shells had already fallen upon the town, the inhabitants of which began to decamp hastily. However, the railway was still intact, and we were expecting the last trains of material from Antwerp. "At all costs"—this is a phrase that recurs very often in orders from the staff, and one which the brigade accepted unmurmuringly—the line was to be protected and the enemy held. Two, three, trains passed, and strange ones they were. They continued to run in until night; the fires were covered up; the engine-drivers never whistled; all that was heard was the muffled pant of the engine, like a great sigh rising from the devastated plains.

That same evening our outposts on the Eessen road were attacked by an armoured car and 200 German cyclists; they repulsed the attack; but we were really too much exposed in our position. The admiral decided that it was imprudent to maintain such a wide front with troops numerically so weak, but which it would take a long time to move off. At Dixmude, on the other hand, where the Yser begins to curve towards the coast, and forms a re-entrant confronting the enemy, there was a position which would permit of a concentric fire from our artillery, particularly favourable to the defensive attitude we were to assume. The considerations which had forced us to extend our front had no longer any weight; all the transports from Antwerp had got in in time. The safety of the Belgian army was assured; its material had reached it, and, with the exception of certain units which had been made prisoners in the evacuation of Antwerp or had been driven into Holland, and the divisions which continued our line to the North Sea, it was in shelter behind the Yser, in touch with the English corps and the army of General d'Urbal. The brigade might therefore very properly concentrate its defensive round Dixmude.

The Belgian command, which had passed into the hands of General Michel, readily accepted these arguments, and the operation was agreed upon for the next day. "The Boches were there twenty-four hours after us," says a sailor's letter. "We hoped they were eight kilometres from the town. We were all dead tired, but standing firm." The evacuation of these dangerous outposts on flat, open ground, where scattered farms, occasional stacks of straw, and the poplars along the roadside were the only available cover, was carried out with very trifling loss, and we at once organised our defences round Dixmude.

"The admiral has cast anchor here," wrote a warrant officer of Servel on October 18. "I don't expect we shall weigh it again just yet."

The image was very appropriate. Dixmude, especially when its eastern outskirts were under water, was not unlike a ship anchored fore and aft at the entrance of an inland sea. But this ship had neither armour plates, quarter-netting, nor portholes. The trenches that had been hastily dug round the town could not have been held against a strong infantry attack; the first rush would have carried them. A whole system of defence had to be organised, and all had to be done in a few hours, actually under the enemy's fire. All honour to the admiral for having attempted it, and for holding on to Dixmude as he would have done to his own ship! No sooner had he recognised the importance of the position than he set to work to increase its defensive value; he was not to be seduced by the feints of the enemy and the temptations offered to beguile him into deploying. Crouching upon the Yser, his head towards the enemy, he only left his lines three times: to support a French cavalry attack upon Thourout, to draw back the enemy, who was concentrating in another direction, and was diverted by fears for Woumen, and finally to co-operate in the recapture of Pervyse and Ramscappelle. But meanwhile, even when he thus detached units and sent them some distance from their base, he kept the whole or a part of his reserves at Dixmude; he clung to his re-entrant—he kept his watch on the Yser.

CHAPTER 5

Dixmude

On October 16, 1914, Dixmude (in Flemish Diksmuiden) numbered about 4,000 inhabitants. The *Guides* call it "a pretty little town," but it was scarcely more than a large village. "It is a kind of Pont-Labbé," wrote one of our sailors, but a Flemish Pont-Labbé, all bricks and tiles, dotted with cafés and nunneries, clean, mystical, sensuous, and charming, especially when the rain ceased for a while, and the old houses, coloured bright green or yellow, smiled at the waters of the canal behind their screen of ancient limes, under a clear sky. From the four points of the horizon long lines of poplars advanced in procession to the fine church of Saint Nicolas, the pride of the place. The graceful fifteenth-century apse was justly praised; but after having admired this, there were further beauties to enjoy in the interior, which contained a good Jouvenet, Jordaens' *Adoration of the Magi*, a well-proportioned font, and one of the most magnificent rood-screens of West Flanders, the contemporary and rival of those of Folgoët and Saint-Etienne-du-Mont.

This stately church, the exquisite Grand' Place of the Hôtel de Ville, the "Roman" bridge of the canal of Handzaeme, the slender silhouette of the Residencia (the house of the Spanish Governors), and five or six other old-time dwellings, with crow-stepped or flexured gables, like the hostelry of *Den Papegaei* (The Parrot), which bore the date of its foundations in huge figures upon its bulging front, hardly sufficed to draw the cosmopolitan tourist tide towards Dixmude. Travellers neglected it; historians ignored it. The capital of an essentially agricultural district, at the confluence of

THE PAPEGAEI INN

two industries, and astride, so to speak, upon the infinity of beet-root-fields and the infinity of meadows to which the Yser serves as the line of demarcation, Dixmude showed a certain animation only on market-days; then it appeared as the metropolis of the vast flat district, streaked with canals and more aquatic than terres-trial, where innumerable flocks and herds pastured under the care of classic shepherds in loose grey coats. The salt marsh-mutton of Dixmude and its butter, which was exported even to England, were famous. A peaceful population, somewhat slow and stolid, ruddy of complexion, husky and deliberate of speech, led lives made up of hard work, religious observance, and sturdy drinking bouts in the scattered farms about the town. The Flemish plains do not breed dreamers. When, like those of Dixmude, such plains are amphibi-ous, half land, half water, they do not, as a rule, stimulate the fight-ing instinct; their inhabitants are absorbed in domestic cares, bat-tling unceasingly for a livelihood with two rival elements.

Such were the only battles that they knew; no invader had ever ventured among them. Invasion, indeed, seemed physically impos-sible. The whole country between the hills of Cassel, Dixmude, and the line of sand-hills along the coast is but a vast *schoore*, a huge polder snatched from the sea, and almost entirely below the sea-level, owing to the deposits of mud left high and dry on the shore. Down to the eleventh century it was still a bay into which the *drakkars* of the Norse pirates might venture. If Dixmude, like Penmarc'h and Pont-Labbé, had retained its maritime character, we might have found on the fronts of its riverside houses the rusty iron rings to which barques were once moored. To safeguard the tenure of this uncertain soil, slowly annexed by centuries of effort, con-quered, but not subdued, and always ready to revert to its former state, it was not enough to thrust back the sea, which would have overflowed it twice a day at high tide; it was further necessary to drain off the fresh water, which streams down into it from the west and the south, mainly from the stiff clay of the Dutch hills, floods the meadows, cuts through the roads, and invades the villages. The struggle is unintermittent. Such country, threatened on every side, is only habitable by virtue of incessant precautions and watchful-ness. The sea is kept under control by Nieuport, with its formidable array of sluices, locks, chambers, water-gates, and cranks; the fresh water, which oozes out on every hand, spangling the rough home-spun of the glebe with diamond pools from the beginning of autumn to long after the end of winter, is dealt with by a methodical and untiring system of drainage directed, under State control, by associations of farmers and landowners (*gardes wateringues*). Hence the innumerable cuttings (*watergands*) along the hedges, the thousands of drains that chequer the soil, the dykes, several metres high, which overhang the rivers—the Yser, the Yperlee, the Kemmel-beck, the Berteartaart, the Vliet, and twenty other unnamed streams of inoffensive aspect—which, when swelled by the autumn rains, become foaming torrents rushing out upon the ancient *schoore* of Dixmude. The roads have to be raised very high in this boundless marsh land, the depressed surface of which is broken only by sparse groups of trees and the roofs of low-lying farms. They are few in number, only just sufficient to ensure communication, and they require constant repair. Torn up by shells and mined by the huge German explosives, the "saucepans" (*marmites*) and "big niggers" (*gros noirs*), as the sailors call them, our company of French and Belgian road-menders had to work day and night throughout the operations to keep them open.

Other roads that meander across the plain are negligible. They are mere tracks, most of which are obliterated when the subter-ranean waters rise in the autumn. For in these regions the water is everywhere: in the air, on the earth, and under the earth, where it appears barely a metre beneath the surface as soon as the crust of soft clay that it raises in blisters is lifted. It rains three days out of four here. Even the north winds, which behead the meagre trees and lay them over in panic-stricken attitudes, bring with them heavy clouds of cold rain gathered in hyborean zones. And when the rain ceases, the mists rise from the ground, white mists, almost solid, in which men and things take on a ghostly aspect. Sometimes indeed the *schoore* lights up between two showers, like a tearful face trying to smile, but such good moments are rare. This is the country of moisture, the kingdom of the waters, of fresh water, that bugbear of sailors. And it was here that fate called upon them to fight, to make their tremendous effort. For nearly four weeks, from October 16 to November 10 (the date of the taking of Dixmude), they, with their admiral, clung desperately to their raft of suffering at the entrance to the delta of marshes, watched over by ancient windmills with shattered wings. One against six, without socks and drawers, under incessant rain, and in mud more cruel than the enemy's shells, they accomplished their task, barring the road to Dunkirk, first ensuring the safety of the Belgian army and then enabling our own Armies of the North to concentrate behind the Yser and dissipate the shock of the enemy's attack. "At the beginning of October," says the *Bulletin des Armées* of November 25, 1914, which sums up the situation very exactly, "the Belgian army quitted Antwerp too much exhausted to take part in any movement.[1] The English were leaving the Aisne for the north; General Castelnau's army had not advanced beyond the south of Arras, and that of General Maudhuy was defending itself from the south of Arras to the south of Lille. Further off we had cavalry, Territorials, and Naval Fusiliers." For the moment at Dixmude, the most exposed point of all, we had only the Fusiliers and a few Belgian detachments, who were putting forth their remaining strength in a supreme effort to co-operate in the defence.

The admiral had said to them: "The task given to you is a solemn and a dangerous one. All your courage is needed. Sacrifice yourselves to save our left wing until reinforcements can come up. Try to hold out for at least *four days*."[2]

At the end of a fortnight the reinforcements had not yet arrived, and the Fusiliers were still "holding out." These men had no illusions as to the fate awaiting them. They knew they were doomed, but they understood the grandeur of their sacrifice. "The post of honour was given to us sailors," wrote Fusilier P., of Audierne, on November 5; "we were to hold that corner at all costs and to die rather than surrender. And indeed we did stand firm, although we were only a handful of men against a force six times as large as ours, with artillery." They numbered exactly 6,000 sailors and 5,000 Belgians, under the command of Colonel (acting General) Meiser, against three German army corps. Their artillery was very insufficient, at least at

---

1. In spite of this, four Belgian divisions held the road from Ypres to Ostend, between Dixmude and Middelkerke, unaided, till October 23, and then the line of the Yser from Dixmude to Nieuport.

2. Pierre Loti, *Illustration* for December 12, 1914.

3. But this was not due to defective organisation. It must be remembered that the brigade was destined for Antwerp, and that unforeseen circumstances had caused it to become a detached corps, operating far from our bases.

THE BÉGUINAGE AT DIXMUDE

the beginning. They had no heavy guns and no aeroplanes,[3] nothing to give them information but the reports of the Belgian cyclists and the approximate estimates of the men in the trenches.

"How many of you were there?" asked a Prussian major who had been taken prisoner, speaking the day after the fall of Dixmude.

"Forty thousand, at least!"

And when he heard that there had been only 6,000 sailors, he wept with rage, muttering:

"Ah! if we had only known!"

CHAPTER 6

The Capture of Beerst

Save for an unimportant suburb beyond the Handzaeme Canal, Dixmude lies entirely on the right bank of the Yser. Nevertheless, our general line of defence on October 16, both up and down stream, went beyond the line traced by the course of the river. From Saint-Jacques-Cappelle to the North Sea, by way of Beerst, Keyem, Leke, Saint-Pierre, etc., little rural settlements but yesterday unknown, drowsing in the gentle Flemish calm, the arc of the circle it described followed, almost throughout its course as far as Slype, the roadside light railway from Ypres to Ostend. The Fusiliers flanked this front from Saint-Jacques to the confluence of the Vliet. The 1st, 2nd, 4th, and 5th Belgian Divisions occupied the rest of the horse-shoe, but the effectives of these reduced divisions had not been made up; some of the regiments had been reduced from 6,000 to 2,000 men; whole companies had melted away. The remnants continued to stand their ground with fine courage. Until when? They had been asked, like our Fusiliers, to hold out for four days, and it was not until October 23, at the end of nine days, that

---

1. The Belgian detachments which co-operated with us in the defence of Dixmude showed themselves no whit inferior to those of the Lower and the Middle Yser, and if we were writing a general account of the operations, and not a chapter in the history of the Naval Brigade, the most elementary justice would require us to give these troops their due for the part they took in the defence. This was so admirable, that the *generalissimo* commissioned General Foch to present General Meiser, whose brigade had specially distinguished itself at Dixmude, with the cravat of Commander of the Legion of Honour, while two of the colours of this brigade, the 11th and the 12th, were decorated by the King and authorised to inscribe the glorious name of the town on their folds. The few hundred (continued on next page)

43

General Grossetti and his reinforcements arrived.[1]

The admiral had divided the defence of Dixmude into two sectors, cut by the road of Caeskerke; the north sector was entrusted to the 1st Regiment, under Commander Delage, the south to the 2nd Regiment, under Commander Varney. His Command Post he established at Caeskerke station, at the junction of the lines of Furnes and Nieuport, keeping only a battalion of the 2nd Regiment at his own disposal. Of the two batteries of the Belgian group, one was sent to the south of the second level crossing of the Furnes railway, the other to the north of Caeskerke. A telephone line connected them with the great flour factory of Dixmude, at the head of the High Bridge. A platform of reinforced cement belonging to this factory provided us with an excellent observatory. The thickness of this mass of concrete, as costly as it was incongruous with the importance of the establishment, but very well adapted for heavy guns, which would command the whole valley of the Yser, did not fail to suggest certain reflections. This was perhaps one of the few instances in which ante-bellum preparations had turned against their authors. The machine-gun company was stationed at the intersection of the roads to Pervyse and Oudecappelle; in the trenches of the Yser we had mainly Belgian troops; finally, to the south, debouching from the forest of Houthulst with four divisions of cavalry, General de Mitry threw out a bold advance post towards Clercken, and relieved us a little on that side, although he was unable to control the German offensive, which began in force at 4 p.m.[2]

The enemy had begun in his customary manner by preparing the ground with his artillery, which from the hollow where it was posted, near Eessen, to the east of Dixmude, rained projectiles upon us from 10 and 15-centimetre guns. Scarcely had the last smoke clouds of the German batteries lifted, when the infantry advanced to the attack. The action was very hot, and was prolonged throughout the night and the morning of the 17th, with violent alterna-

Senegalese who reinforced the Fusiliers towards the end also gave us very active and brilliant support, on which, for similar reasons, we have not insisted in our narrative.
2. It was General de Mitry's corps which guarded the Yser towards Loo. With magnificent audacity, General d'Urbal had thrown it upon the forest of Houthulst before he had all his forces in hand. Here it was to dislodge the Germans, and then march upon Thourout and Roulers while Sir Henry Rawlinson marched upon Menin.

The Bridge and Flour Factory

tions of advance and retreat. The enemy, anxious to deal a decisive blow, came on in compact masses, in which our machine-guns and rifle fire tore bloody breaches. These mobile bastions wavered for a few seconds, filled up the breaches, and then returned to the charge in the same close formation as before. No network of barbed wire protected the approach to our trenches; most of them had neither roofs nor parapets. In these haphazard defences, successful resistance depended solely on the intrepidity of the men and the skill of the commander. Certain "elements" were taken, retaken, lost, and retaken again. But as a whole our line held; the enemy failed to break through it. At dawn, discouraged, he suspended his attack, but, like a dog who makes off growling, he never ceased shelling us till 11 a.m. "After this," notes Fusilier B., "all noise ceased. Dixmude has not suffered much. The damage caused by the shells is insignificant." True, the enemy had not yet received his heavy artillery.

We profited by the respite granted us to repair the trenches of the outskirts, which were somewhat damaged, and begin the organisation of the others. This work, indeed, was resumed whenever there was a lull, but it was carried on chiefly at night, and in the morning, from 5 to 9 o'clock, until the mists lifted. At this hour and the coming of light the German batteries generally awoke. We had not enough guns to reply efficaciously to the enemy. The brigade was therefore greatly rejoiced by the reinforcements it received during the day of the 17th: five batteries of the 3rd Regiment of Belgian Artillery (Colonel de Weeschouwer), which, added to the Pontus group, gave the defenders of Dixmude the respectable total of 72 guns. Unhappily their range was not very great, and the metal of which they were made was not strong enough to bear the strain of our .75 shells. Such as they were, however, our front was in much better case when they had been distributed from Caeskerke to Saint-Jacques-Cappelle. The admiral, who wished to direct their operations himself, had these batteries connected by telephone with his quarters; a battle is directed from a study-table nowadays. Nevertheless, he gave a standing order that the batteries were to open fire instantly, whether by day or night, on the approaches to Dixmude, whenever rifle fire or the sound of machine-guns indicated that an infantry attack threatened our trenches.

The check received on October 16 had perhaps made the enemy more cautious. He had allowed us breathing time in the afternoon of the 17th, and he gave us a quiet day on Sunday, the 18th. Only two or three cavalry patrols were reported near Dixmude, and these were rapidly dispersed by a few salvoes. That day, too, our Fusiliers had a pleasant surprise. A tall, silent officer, with serious eyes, in a closely buttoned black dolman, came to visit the trenches of the Yser with the admiral. His inspection seemed satisfactory to him. He pressed the admiral's hand, and when he had regained the river bank, he paused a moment, gazing at the triangle of marshes, all that remained to him of his kingdom. It was Albert I.[3]

Other news from the front arrived, and gave us confidence. In spite of the fall of Lille, our Armies of the North had taken the offensive with marked success from Roye to the Lys. Orders had come from the English headquarters to the 1st Corps to concentrate at Ypres, whence it was to attempt to advance towards Bruges.[4] This strategic movement had even been initiated, and the French cavalry which had just seized Clercken might be considered the advance guard of Sir Douglas Haig's corps. It asked the admiral to support it in flank, to enable it to push on to Zarren and Thourout. He at once sent forward Commander de Kerros with a battalion of the 1st Regiment and two Belgian armoured cars towards Eessen.[5] The road was free; it was strewn with the carcases of dead horses, and even with dead soldiers, as if there had been a precipitate retreat. The enemy seemed to have evaporated. But the church of Eessen, which he had turned into a stable, just as afterwards he turned the church of Vladsloo into a cesspool, with the immemorial Teuton taste for sacrilege, showed evidences of his recent passage. These tracks of the beast did not, however, tell us which way he had gone. Several roads lay open to him. It seemed most probable that, hearing of the movement of the French cavalry, he was retiring upon Bruges by way of Wercken or Vladsloo. Taking his chance, Commander de Kerros had installed himself to await

3. 28 "He's a model king: I saw him visiting the trenches; he's a man, if you like." (Letter of a sailor, A. C., October 30.)
4. *Cf.* Sir John French's report. As is well known, this movement, which began on October 21, was stopped on the line Zonnebeke-Saint-Julien-Langermack-Bixschoote.
5. Commander de Kerros had made an offensive reconnaissance in this direction the day before.

the morning, while two Turco regiments,[6] which had been placed at the admiral's disposal and ensured his liaison with the main body operating on Thourout, set out as foragers towards Bovekerke and the woods of Couckelaere. Morning dawned, and the execution of the French plan seemed about to be realised normally, when a terrible thrust by the enemy at a wholly unexpected point suddenly upset all calculations.

In reality the Germans had not retreated at all, or rather they had only retired to come into touch again under more favourable conditions. Knowing the sort of reception that awaited them at Dixmude, they had decided to try another point on the front, in the hope that "the little Belgians" would be easier to deal with than the "young ladies with red pompons." About 9 o'clock on the morning of the 19th they threw themselves in three simultaneous leaps, at Leke, Keyem, and Beerst, upon the thin Belgian line, which staggered under the shock. The question was whether we should be able to reinforce it in time. If it were broken, the road would lie open to the Yser, the Yser would perhaps be seized, and Dixmude taken in the rear. The admiral did not hesitate; the whole brigade should go if necessary. He sent forward two of his reserve battalions by forced marches on the road to Ostend, another, under Commander Mauros, towards Vladsloo and Hoograde in flank. The artillery supported the movement, which began at 10 o'clock. But we did not know whether Keyem and Beerst were in the hands of the Belgians or of the Germans, and in this uncertainty we dared not open fire upon them. The two villages were wrapped in ominous silence. Commander Jeanniot and Commander Pugliesi-Conti, who were marching upon Keyem with the first and second battalions of the 2nd Regiment, made their arrangements accordingly. While the sixth company of the second battalion advanced towards Keyem, with Lieutenant Pertus, the fifth company, under Lieutenant de Maussion de Candé, received orders to make for Beerst. De Maussion put his company into line of sections in fours. On approaching the village he was received by a salvo of machine-guns. The Germans were entrenched in the houses and the church, whence they poured a withering fire upon our troops. The attack was made peculiarly difficult by the nature of the ground,

6. Under Colonel du Jonchay. Abd-el-Kader's grandson was with them.

BELGIAN ARMOURED CAR RECONNOITRING IN THE PLAIN OF DIXMUDE

which was completely flat, and afforded no cover save the irrigation ditches and a few leafless hedges; the only possible method of advance was crawling. We lost a good many men in this deploying manoeuvre, so ill adapted to the impulsive nature of sailors; every head that was raised became a target. De Maussion, who had stood up to inspect the enemy's position, was struck down. Every moment one of our men rolled over among the beetroots. Would the charge never sound? It would, but not yet. Pertus fell first, his leg shattered at the moment when he was carrying a group of farms close to Keyem; Lieutenant Hébert was sent with the eighth company to support him. But the ditches on the road were already occupied by the men of the first battalion, and Hébert had to cut across fields to avoid this encumbered road. The fire directed against us had become very hot. It took us in flank, and we ran the risk of being wiped out before we had reached our objective. The Hébert company accordingly swerved to the right, and marched to the edge of the woods and the houses situated between Beerst and Keyem, where the enemy's artillery and infantry seemed to be posted.[7] Hébert took up a position in a farm with the third section; Second-Lieutenant de Blois and Boatswain Fossey with the first and second sections deployed to act as marksmen, facing the wood. Creeping from hedge to hedge and from *watergand* to *watergand*, supported by Lieutenant de Roncy's machine-guns, they arrived to within 500 metres of the enemy's position in connection with Commander Jeanniot, who had arrived at the same point on the left by a similar manoeuvre.

"I think this is our moment," said the commander.

"Forward!" cried De Blois to his men.

Fossey gave the same order; the two sections sprang out of their temporary trenches under a hail of bullets. Fossey was killed, De Blois severely wounded in the head and leg.[8] The rest of the sections found their way to the farm where Hébert was making an attempt to check the enemy's counter-attack by fire from the loopholes that had been stopped up by the former occupants of the upper storeys,

7. The woods in question were the Praetbosch.

8. Under the pseudonym of D'Avesnes, the Comte de Blois has published some notes of travel, various stories, and a naval novel, *La Vocation*, remarkable for their delicate sentiment and subtlety of analysis. It is bare justice to record here the gallantry of Quartermaster Echivant, who carried his wounded officer off to the rear under a heavy fire.

but which he had succeeded in opening. His exertions were cut short by an invisible battery, which broke down the walls, wounded his two lieutenants, and obliged him to fall back. He himself was wounded twice as he crept through the ditches.[9] Second-Lieutenant de Réau, who came out of cover to advance, had his shoulder shattered. The casualties in the Jeanniot battalion, whose sections continued the attack, leaving 110 of their number on the field, soon became so serious that they had to be brought back to the rear. It was then that the "colonel" of the 2nd Regiment, rallying the remnants of the companies engaged, and continuing to cover them towards Keyem, massed his forces, put himself at their head, and, after crawling up to within two hundred yards of the position, hurled himself upon Beerst. His example electrified his men. This time they would have allowed themselves to be cut to pieces sooner than give way. Some of them had thrown off their great-coats that they might move more freely. The old corsair blood was boiling in their veins. It was no longer a charge, but a boarding of the enemy's ships, and, as in the heroic days, the first who sprang upon the deck, pistols in hand and sword between teeth, was the chief. The whole crew rushed after the "colonel" of the 2nd Regiment, who had become Commander Varney again. But as soon as one house was captured the next had to be taken by assault. Nevertheless, the attack progressed. To keep it in heart, the admiral sent forward the second battalion of the 1st Regiment, under Commander Kerros, to support it, and withdrew the sorely tried Jeanniot battalion to Dixmude. The Mauros battalion debouched simultaneously from Vladsloo, whence it had dislodged the enemy, with the help of the Belgian Brigade and their armoured cars; the 5th Allied Division prolonged the fighting line to the right and in the rear. The effects of this successful tactical arrangement were at once felt: the enemy, who had brought his artillery into action, was groping about in search of the guns we had brought

9. "We were able to get away by creeping through the ditches, but picked marksmen concealed in the trees decimated us. Suddenly my left arm began to hurt me horribly. A bullet had torn the muscles from elbow to wrist. A second bullet, aimed at my heart, went through a note-block and a war manual, and was stopped by my pocket-book. I fell. My men carried me off under fire. The last thing I remember seeing was a captive balloon which was hovering over the woods directing the fire of the enemy's battery." (R. Kimley, *op. cit.*) M. Hébert is the famous inventor of the system of naval athletics which bears his name.

along to the north of Dixmude; at 5 o'clock in the afternoon we were in possession of Beerst. The bayonets were able to take a rest; they had done yeoman's service; in the streets and in the farmyards, the ground was paved with corpses. But night was falling. The admiral, who had come up to the firing line, ordered Commander Varney to put the approaches to the village into a state of defence at once in view of a possible offensive return of the enemy. The men obeyed gaily; they were still in the full flush of their costly victory.[10] They had scarcely begun to wield their picks, when a counter-order came from Belgian headquarters: we were to fall back upon our former positions! At 11 o'clock that night the brigade returned to its quarters at Caeskerke and Saint-Jacques-Cappelle. The horizon was aflame behind it: Hoograde, Beerst, and Vladsloo had been re-occupied by the enemy, who were "setting the red cock up" on the roofs (*i.e.*, firing them).

---

10. "Monday, October 19, bayonet attack on Beerst. Several officers killed and wounded." (Note-book of Second-Lieutenant X.) "We have been fighting for five days," wrote Second-Lieutenant Gautier on October 22. "The day before yesterday we resumed the offensive. It was a bit stiff. Don't be too much upset by the casualty lists. I should not have said anything about them, but as you will see them in the papers, I would rather tell you of them myself. Le Douget, who was in the training companies at Lorient, was killed at Ghent; De Maussion was killed the day before yesterday; Hébert, Pertus, and De Mons are wounded." In his note-book, under date of the 18th, Gautier adds the names of Second-Lieutenants de Blois and de Roussille as among the wounded. He gives some interesting details of the affair itself. A little incident reported by the Abbé Le H. bears witness to the heroism and self-sacrifice of the men. "It was at Beerst. A quartermaster had his leg broken by a bullet in the temporary trench he was occupying with his company. He went on fighting. His comrades were obliged to fall back under a tremendous fire. He refused to be carried away, and crawled into a ditch, where he killed three Germans who came creeping up to take him prisoner. Fortunately, a young marine, who had been trained by him at Lorient, could not make up his mind to abandon the quartermaster. By dint of extraordinary efforts, he managed to reach him and succeeded in dragging him some three hundred yards to a house, where he left him under shelter. As he left this house he himself was wounded in the arm by a bullet. Night was falling. He came to the dressing-station to have his wound attended to. I was there. He told me his story with such infectious emotion that I proposed he should act as guide to two stretcher-bearers and myself for the purpose of bringing in the quartermaster. Without a moment's hesitation, he set out in front of us, heedless of the very real danger. After a difficult pilgrimage over open ground swept by the German machine-guns, we were lucky enough to find the quartermaster and to bring him back into our lines. I notified the conduct of these two brave fellows to the commanding officer that same evening, and I hope they received the reward they deserved."

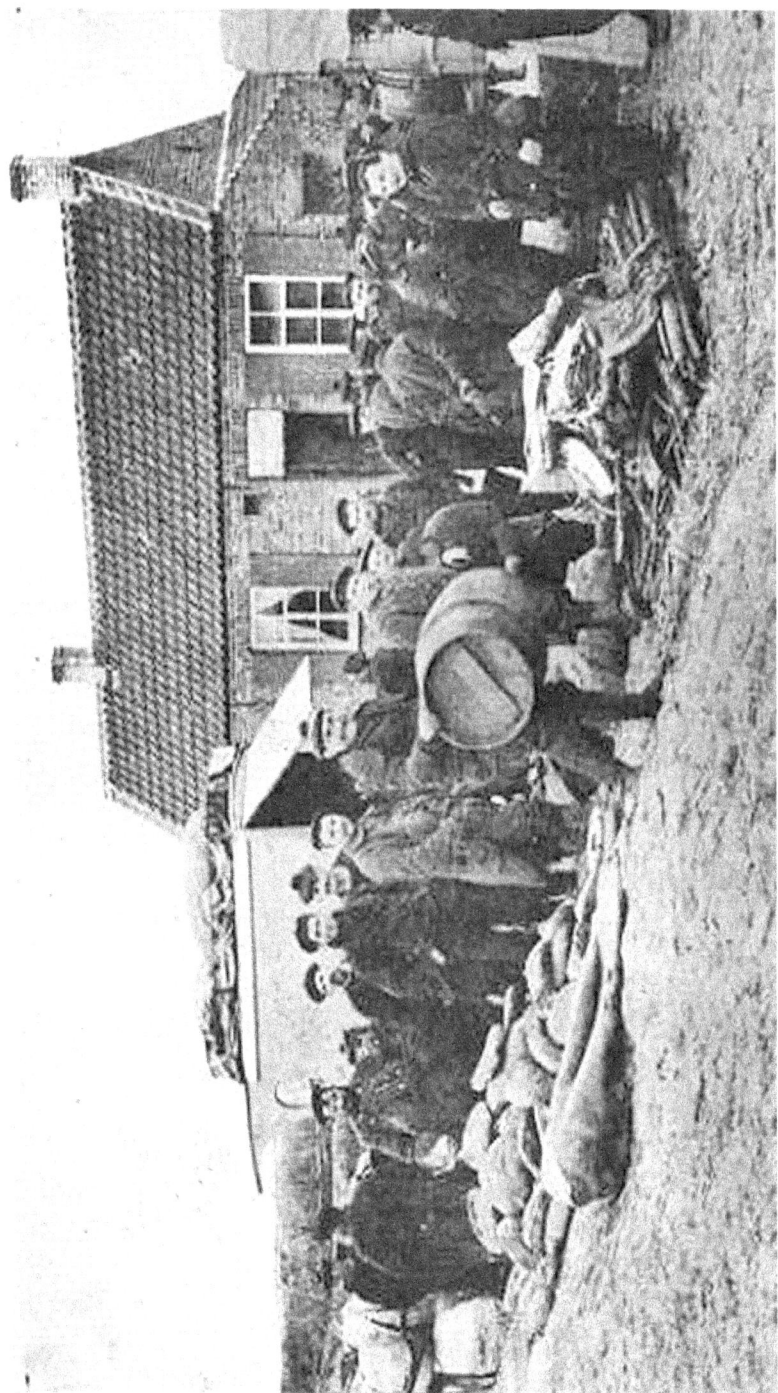

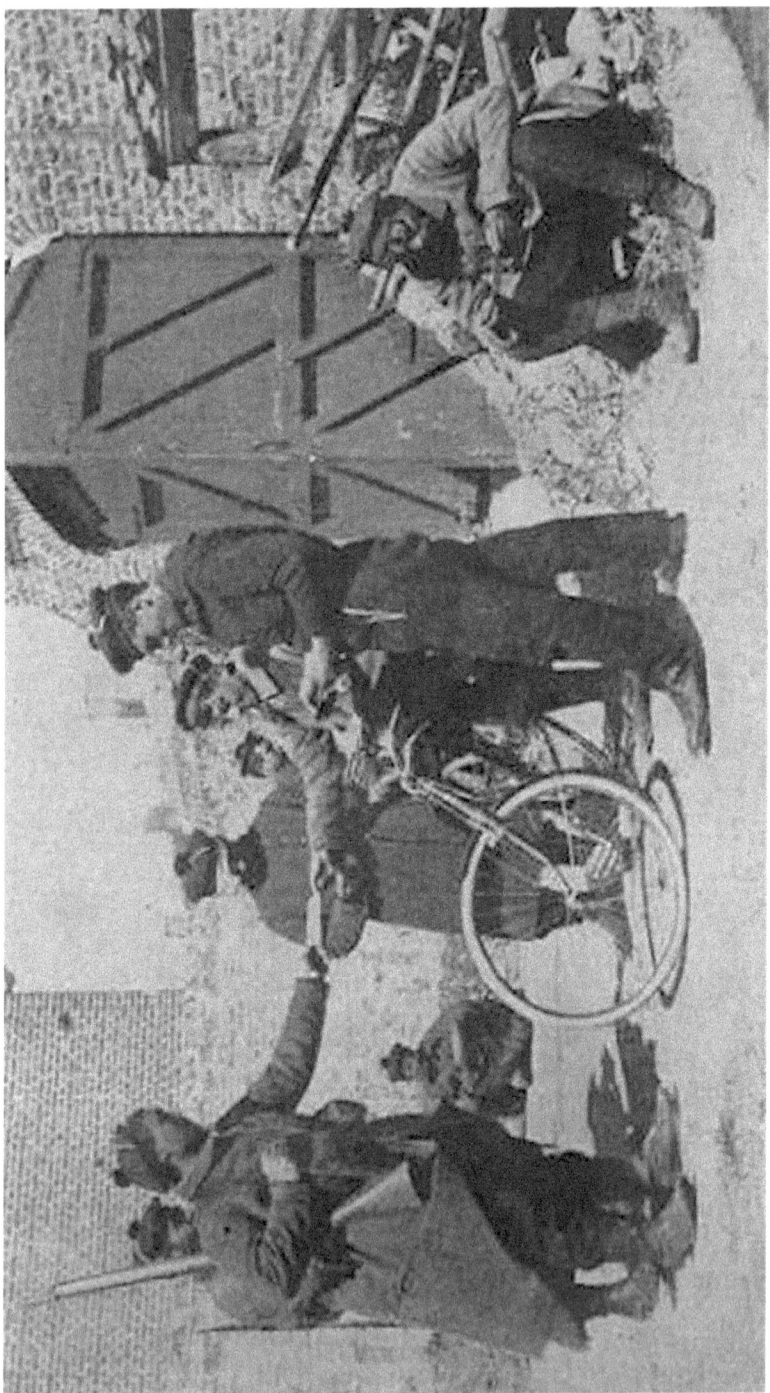

DIXMUDE 1914. — Les Belges arrêtent les Allemands sur le vieux pont de l'Yser.

CHAPTER 7

The First Effects of the Bombardment

The Belgian headquarters staff had probably decided that its front on the Ostend road was too ex-centric, and that the line of the Yser would form a more solid epaulement. And in this case our diversion on Beerst was not quite useless, since it had secured the orderly retreat of the Belgian troops; but, on the other hand, as a result of this diversion and of the reinforcement of the German troops, De Mitry had been unable to maintain himself at Thourout; the Turcos had returned to Loo, and the rest of the French cavalry was obliged to follow the movement. The whole of the ground in front of Dixmude lay open to the enemy, who, reinforced by fresh contingents and the heavy artillery from Antwerp, released by the capitulation of the city, prepared in all security to renew the attack upon our positions in combination with a parallel action on the lines of the Lower and Middle Yser. In order to understand clearly what follows, it will be necessary to remember that the defence of Dixmude and of the Yser, and, in the event of the forcing of the Yser, the defence of the railway from Caeskerke to Nieuport were closely connected, and that Pervyse and Ramscappelle lead to Furnes as well as Dixmude, Pollinchove, or Loo.

A new disposition of the Allied forces was required under the new conditions. During the night of October 19 the Belgian Meiser Brigade passed under the admiral's orders; on the 20th at 11 o'clock the first "saucepan" fell upon Dixmude. "Up to this date," writes Captain X., "77 shrapnel, with their queer caterwaulings, were the only presents the enemy had sent us. But during the course of the 20th the big shells began to rain upon us, and their first objective was, of course, the church. At the fifth or sixth the beautiful building was on fire."[1] And we had no observer there. In preparation for the bombardment, we had worked all night at the trenches. Those nearest to the enemy had been provided with parapets and barbed wire entanglements, dug down to a depth of I metre 70 cm., and strongly roofed. But all the internal defences remained to be organised, notably the railway embankment, where the "big niggers" were falling in showers. One evening when his company was in reserve, after forty-eight hours in the trenches, Lieutenant A. was ordered to take up a position there. He had been on guard there three nights before; he knew by experience how dangerous this spot was, and, less for his own sake than for the 250 men under his charge, he thought it his duty to speak out.

"There are no trenches on the railway slope, Commander," he remarked to Captain V.

"I know that."

"Oh, very well, sir."

"And smiling to encourage his men," added the eye-witness who reported this dialogue, "he went off to a post as exposed as a glacis."

With such officers, Dixmude was better defended than if it had had a triple line of blockhouses. The men, who were worthy of their leaders, had soon grown used to the racket of the shells. The damage they do is not in proportion to the noise they make, "for one can see them coming, and they are heralded by a creaking sound, as of ungreased pulleys,"[2] wrote a marine to his family, adding ingenuously: "All the same, anyone who wants to hear guns has only to come here." Indeed, the noise was stupendous: 420, 305, and 77 were thundering in unison. As we had no heavy artillery to reply, we had to wait patiently for the inevitable attack

1. *Cf.* Dr. Caradec, *op. cit.*, also the note-book and letters of Second-Lieutenant Gautier: "11 o'clock, the church on fire.... Sailors are queer creatures. Yesterday, while the church was being bombarded they exclaimed: 'Oh, the brutes! I wish I could get hold of one of them and break his jaw!' This morning we took a wounded prisoner. There was not a word of hatred, not an insult, as he passed. Two sailors were helping him along. He said: 'Good-day. War is a terrible thing.' And our men answered. They are more French than they think."

2. "At first the big shells give one a very unpleasant sensation, but one gets used to them, and learns to guess from the whistling noise they make where they are likely to fall." (Second-Lieutenant Gautier's note-book.)

which follows after the ground is cleared. Then the 72-m. guns of our six groups would be able to have their say. Unfortunately on our right the ravages caused in the Belgian trenches by the storm of German artillery had made it impossible for our allies to hold their position; this being duly notified in time, the admiral sent four of our companies to replace them. Scarcely were they installed, when the German attack began. Sure of themselves and of victory, they had adopted the close formation of their first onslaught, with machine-guns in the rear, the veterans on the two wings, the conscripts in the centre and in front, the latter with rapt, ecstatic faces, the former swelling with the pride of former victories, all united by the same patriotic ideal, marching rhythmically, and singing hymns to the national God. The majority were young men, hardly more than boys. Later, in the trenches, when the marines fell upon them, they knelt down, clasping their hands, weeping, and begging for quarter. But here, in the excitement of the *mêlée*, elbow to elbow and sixteen ranks deep, they had but one colossal and ferocious soul. They were swinging along with a slightly undulating movement when the fire of our machine-guns struck them, true sons of those other barbarians who linked themselves together with chains, that they might form a solid block in death or in victory. An aroma of alcohol, ether, and murder preceded them, as it had been the breath of the blood-stained machine. Our men allowed them to approach within a hundred yards. To the shouts of *Vorwärts!* ("Forward!") from the enemy's ranks we answered abruptly by the orders "Independent fire! Continuous fire!" given by officers and petty officers. Behind their parapets, amidst the buzz of bullets and the bursting of shrapnel, the marines did not miss a single shot. "We'll do for you!" yelled the gunners, catching the contagious fever of battle. The Germans came on steadily, but the mass was no longer solid. The dislocated machine was working with difficulty. It uttered its death-rattle at the foot of the trenches in the network of barbed wire where the survivors had rolled over. At 8 o'clock in the evening three blasts on a whistle, strident as a factory hooter, put an end to the work of the monstrous organism.

The battle had been raging for six hours in the night. Once more we were the victors, but at what a price! Dixmude, which the enemy's heavy artillery had battered incessantly during the attack, was not yet the "heap of pebbles and ashes," the line of blackened stones, it was presently to become, but its death agony had begun. Innumerable houses had been gutted. The entire quarter round the church was on fire. The rain, heavy as it was, could not extinguish the flames kindled by incendiary bombs. A projectile struck the belfry of Saint Nicolas at the hour of the Angelus; the great bell, mortally wounded, uttered a kind of dying groan, the vibrations of which quivered long in space. "Poor Dixmude!" cried a sailor; "your passing bell is tolling." Happily, the population was no longer on the spot. The Burgomaster had given the signal of exodus, and all had obeyed it, stricken to the heart, with the exception of the Carmelites and some dozen laggards and stubborn spirits, such as the old beadle described by M. T'Serstevens, who lived in a little gabled house with barred windows on the Grand' Place, and who, pipe in mouth, used to bring the keys of the church to visitors. He mumbled the rude Flemish dialect of the coast, and was tanned by the sea-wind. "The church, the house, the Place, the old man, were all in harmony: all embodied the unique soul of Mother Flanders," and all were destroyed at the same time; the old man was unable to disengage himself from his house, of which he seemed but a more animated stone than the rest.

In spite of the retreat of the enemy, the four companies of marines had been left at their posts as a precautionary measure. An intermittent fusillade to the north of the Yser during the night suggested a renewed offensive. The only attack of any moment took place at 3 o'clock in the morning, "but we repulsed it easily," notes the Marine R., "for in our covered trenches we are invulnerable." Disappointed, the enemy turned again towards the town, which he began to bombard once more at dawn. It chanced that the weather had cleared. The *schoore* smiled; the larks were singing; weary of lowing for their sheds, or already resigned to their forsaken condition, the cattle were ruminating in the sun:[3] and the interminable line of canals, the silvery surfaces of the *watergands*, shone softly on the brown velvet of the marsh. The

---

3. "The cattle are running about on all the roads and in all the fields. No one attends to them." (Letter of the Marine E.T.) See also below, De Nanteuil.

THE PARISH CHURCH AFTER THE FIRST DAYS OF THE BOMBARDMENT

sky, however, as says the Psalmist, armed itself with thunders and lightnings. The bombardment became particularly violent in the afternoon. An officer writes:

At given moments the whole town seemed about to crumble. The Germans had first attacked it with 10-centimetre guns, then with 15, and then with 21-centimetre; but as this was no good, they determined to finish off these infernal sailors in grand style with their 305 and 420-mm.[4]

Our reserves in Dixmude were of course sorely tried by this terrible fire, which it was difficult to locate and still more difficult to silence with defective guns. To add to the complexities of the situation, we learned suddenly that at 4 o'clock the enemy had taken one of the trenches on the outskirts to the south of the town. Surprised by an attack in force, the Belgian section which occupied it gave way after a spirited resistance, involving the supporting section of marines in their rear in their retreat. Only Lieutenant Cayrol remained at his post, revolver in hand, to enable his men to carry off the machine-guns.[5] Three companies at once crept along towards the captured trenches after our guns had cleared the approaches a little.

One of the actors in this scene writes:

We tried our hands as marksmen and while the Boches were trying to re-form, before they had recovered from their surprise, we fired into them at 50 metres, and then charged them with the bayonet. You should have seen them run like hares, throwing away their arms and all their equipment. What a raid it was, five to six hundred dead and wounded and forty prisoners, among them three officers! We reoccupied the trenches, and I spent the night in the company of a dead Belgian and a wounded German, who, when he woke up, exclaimed: 'Long

---

4. *Cf.* Dr. Caradec, *op. cit.*

5. The note which furnishes this information as to the heroic conduct of Lieutenant Cayrol adds: "Received a bullet in the middle of his forehead. Brought into the dressing-station by his men, where he gave an account of the incident and of the bravery of his men. He would not consent to be removed until he had been assured that his machine-guns were saved. Has come back to the front."

live France!' lest we should run him through. When day came, and we could behold our work ... (Here an interval. A shell burst just over my head, smashed a rifle, and threw a handful of earth in my face. It was slightly unpleasant. I continue.) It was a pretty sight. All day long stretcher-bearers were picking up the dead and wounded, while we continued to fire from time to time. All the wounded we have picked up are young men, sixteen to twenty years old, of the last levy. The next night there was a repetition of these experiences, only this time it was the northern trenches that failed. As always, it was the sailors who had to recapture them. For lack of available forces, we were obliged to send two companies of the 2nd Regiment, which had been set aside to act as reliefs; they put matters right by a little bayonet play.

A second quartermaster writes:

You might have supposed that after this dance we had claims to a turn at the buffet. Not a bit of it! My company had been set aside for relief, and it carried out the relief. It would be untrue to say that we are not all a bit blown; but we are holding out all the same. We called the roll; there were some who did not answer to their names, and who will not see their mammies again.... If only we could move about a bit to stretch our legs! But we are packed together in the mud like sardines in their oil. In the morning the hurly-burly began again, first a few shrapnel, then from 12 to 1 a perfect whirl-wind of shells of every imaginable calibre. How they lavish their munitions, the brutes!

This defence of the Yser was, to quote the words of Dr. L., "an eternal Penelope's web." Scarcely had it been mended, when the fabric gave way at another point. Thanks to the reinforcements the enemy had received, his pressure became more violent every day. Reduced to impotence on the flank of the defence, where the vigorous attitude of our sailors deluded him into the belief that he had to deal with superior numbers, the foe pushed forward his centre. He succeeded in driving in a wedge on October 22,[6] occupying

6. Second-Lieutenant Gautier's note-book has the (continued on next page)

Tervaete and gaining a footing "for the first time on the left bank of the Yser."[7] The 1st Belgian Division, thrown back, but not broken, sent us word that it would attack next day, supported by our artillery. We were further to send them one or two of our reserve battalions. But the next day Dixmude and our outer trenches were so furiously bombarded that we required our total strength to resist. The Germans were evidently using their biggest calibres, 21 and perhaps 28-cm. In spite of all this, their infantry could not get into our trenches. We had a few casualties, both killed and wounded, among the latter Commander Delage, "colonel" of the 2nd Regiment, who, when his wound was dressed, would not stay in the ambulance, but resumed his command before he was cured. But things had not been going so well with our allies at Tervaete. Checked in a first attempt, a second and more vigorous counter-attack succeeded in driving the Germans into the river or upon the other bank; but this, as the *Courrier de l'Armée Belge* admitted, "was a transitory success, for the same evening German reinforcements renewed the attack, and carried Tervaete." Our artillery had done its best under the circumstances; but, shouted down by the clamour of the big German guns, it was not able to keep up the conversation. "We still have nothing but the little Belgian guns," wrote Second-Lieutenant M. on the morning of the 22nd. "However, we are promised two batteries of short 155-mm. and two of long 120-mm. They arrived in the course of the evening. That's all right! Now perhaps we shall be able to have a little talk with the Boches!"

But was it not already too late? Dixmude was impregnable only so long as it was not taken in the rear; and the enemy, hav-

following under date of October 22: "Cannonade still lively. One of our convoys blown to pieces." The incident took place the day before, and is evidently identical with that mentioned by Second-Lieutenant X. under date of October 21: "Intensive shelling, a good deal of damage. De Mons and Demarquay, naval lieutenants, wounded. The church on fire. In the afternoon a German airship spotted an important convoy (provisions, ambulances, munitions, etc.) on the road from Caeskerke to Oudecappelle. The convoy was shelled."

7. *Courrier de l'Armée Belge*. The pressure, says this official *communiqué*, was very strong, had been very strong ever since the 20th. On that day "a furious bombardment by guns of every calibre had been kept up upon the Belgian lines. A farm situated in the front of the 2nd Division was taken by the Germans, retaken by the Belgians, and again lost." On the 21st a German attack upon Schoorbakke, combined with an attack upon Dixmude, failed signally. But the Belgians were becoming worn out.

ing finally occupied the whole of the Tervaete loop, was gradually penetrating into the valley of the Yser. The last news was that he had arrived at Stuyvekenskerke. The 42nd French Infantry Division, under General Grossetti, which was to replace the 2nd Belgian Division, now reduced to a fourth of its original strength, on the Yser, had not yet had time to come up into line. At Dixmude itself the pressure was formidable; shells were falling on us from every side, from Vladsloo, from Eessen, and from Clercken, whither the Germans had removed their heavy artillery. And at the same time the enemy's infantry attacked our trenches regularly at intervals of an hour, with the stubbornness of a ram butting at an obstacle, preceding every attack by a few big shells. It looked as if they were trying to divert our attention, to prevent us from noticing what was going on down below in the hollow of the Yser, where a grey surge seemed to be seething, and where the *schoore* appeared to be moving towards Oud Stuyvekenskerke. But the movement had not escaped the admiral, who was watching it from Caeskerke. Whence had these troops come—from Tervaete, from Stuyvekenskerke, or elsewhere? We could not say, and it mattered little. At whatever point a breach had been made in the defences of the Middle Yser, the German tide had crept up to us: Dixmude was turned.

In this, the most critical situation in which the brigade had yet been placed, the admiral had only his reserves and a few Belgian contingents at his disposal. To bar the way to the bridges of Dixmude, Commander Rabot, with a battalion, hurried to the support of the left wing of the front. Commander Jeanniot, with another battalion, crept up towards Oud Stuyvekenskerke, to support the Belgians, having received orders to occupy the outskirts at least. The manoeuvre was a peculiarly difficult one to carry out, under a raking fire, and with men already dropping with fatigue and perishing with cold and drowsiness. But these men were sailors. Marine F., of the island of Sein writes:

> On October 24 we had spent a day and a night in the first line. That night we had two men killed in our trench and four wounded by a shell, and we were going to the rear for a little well-earned rest. Scarcely had we swallowed our coffee,

when the order came to clear the decks, as we say on board ship, and shoulder our knapsacks. When we got nearer, the bullets began to whistle. We crawled on all fours over the exposed ground, without a shred of cover. Those who ventured to raise their heads were at once wounded, though we could see nothing of the Germans. We got so accustomed to the bullets whizzing past our ears that we lost all fear and advanced steadily.

That day, however, our worthy marine got no further. In the thick of the firing, a bullet broke his leg, and sent him rolling over into a pool. But as he was a Breton, with a great respect for Madame Saint Anne of Le Porzic, he made a vow that if he got off without further damage, he would give her on the day of her "pardon" a fine white marble *ex-voto*, with "Thanks to Saint Anne for having preserved me" engraved upon it.

All his comrades were not so fortunate, and at the close of the day the majority of the officers engaged, notably those of the second and third battalions of the 1st Regiment, were *hors de combat*. But we held the outskirts of Oud Stuyvekenskerke; Commander Jeanniot and the Belgian troops, with Commander Rabot, had succeeded, according to the admiral's instructions, in forming a line of defence facing north, which bid defiance to the enemy's attacks. Moreover, heavy as our losses were, they were nothing as compared with those of the Germans. The following dispirited comments were found in the note-book of a German officer of the 202nd Regiment of Infantry killed at Oud Stuyvekenskerke the following day:

> We are losing men on every hand, and our losses are out of all proportion to the results obtained. Our guns do not succeed in silencing the enemy's batteries; our infantry attacks are ineffectual: they only lead to useless butchery. Our losses must be enormous. My colonel, my major, and many other officers are dead or wounded. All our regiments are mixed up together; the enemy's merciless fire enfilades us. They have a great many *francs-tireurs* with them.
>
> *Francs-tireurs!* We know what the Germans understand by this

term, which merely means skilled marksmen.[8] If our sailors had not been so hitherto, the night attack which crowned this tragic day showed that they had become so. The attack was unprecedented and of unparalleled fury. Between 5 p.m. and midnight we and the Belgians had to repulse no less than fifteen attacks on the south sector of the defence, and eleven on the north and east sectors. The enemy charged with the cries of wild beasts, and for the first time our men saw the brutish face of War. The next day, as soon as the mists lifted, the battle began again along the whole line. The town was bombarded, the outer trenches, the trenches of the Yser, and, above all, the railway station at Caeskerke, where the admiral was. He had to resign himself to a change of quarters without gaining much in the way of safety. The enemy had spies in Dixmude itself. "The houses of the staff were spotted one after the other as soon as any change was made," writes an officer; "and every day at noon, when we were at our midday meal, we were greeted by four big shells. Scarcely had a heavy battery been in position for five minutes, when the position became untenable: a man in a tree a hundred yards off was quietly making signals."

In the north alone a certain relaxation of the enemy's pressure was noted. Abandoning the attempt to turn Dixmude by way of Oud Stuyvekenskerke, the Germans seemed anxious to push on to Pervyse and Ramscappelle, from which they were only separated by the embankment of the Nieuport railway. The Grossetti Division endeavoured to stop the way with the remnant of the Belgian divisions, and sent a battalion of the 19th Chasseurs to relieve us at Oud Stuyvekenskerke. Commander Jeanniot at once went into the reserve trenches of the sector. His men were utterly worn out. The companies which had occupied the outer trenches of the defence, and which had not been relieved for four days, were not less exhausted. The enemy's fire on the Dixmude front never ceased, the town heaved and shuddered at every blast, the paving stones were dislodged, every window was shattered, houses were perpetually crumbling into heaps of rubble, and after each explosion immense

---

8. R. Kimley (*op. cit.*), quoting Lieutenant Hébert, offers another and perhaps a more acceptable explanation. In their dark blue overcoats and their caps with red pompons, the sailors looked strange to the Germans, who took them for *francs-tireurs*. The terror they inspired was aggravated by this idea.

THE TOWN-HALL AND BELFRY AFTER THE FIRST DAYS OF THE BOMBARDMENT

spirals of black smoke rose as high as 100 metres above the craters made by the shells. "During the night of Sunday, the 25th," notes the Marine R., on duty with Commander Mauros, of the third battalion, "we were thrice obliged to evacuate the houses in which we were, as they fell in upon us." "Dixmude is gradually crumbling away," wrote Lieutenant S. on the following day. The Carmelites had left on October 21; their monastery, where the chaplains of the brigade[9] continued to officiate imperturbably, had received three big shells during the day. The belfry still held, but it had lost three of its turrets, and the charming Gothic façade of the town-hall had a great hole in the first storey. It looked like a piece of lace through which a clumsy fist had been thrust. The enemy did not even spare our ambulances. "A chapel in the middle of the town, protected by the Red Cross (Hospital of St. John), was shelled from end to end," says Marine F. A., of Audierne; "not a single one of the surrounding churches and belfries has been left standing."[10] The worst of it was that our forces, greatly tried in the last encounters, no longer sufficed for the exigencies of the defence. We had to be making constant appeals to the depots. The winter rains had begun, flooding the trenches. If it had not been for the heavy cloth overcoats insisted on by a far-seeing administration, the men would have died of cold. Many who through carelessness, or in the hurry of departure, had left their bags at Saint-Denis, went shivering on guard in cotton vests, their bare feet in ragged slippers. All their letters are full of imprecations against the horrible water that was benumbing them, diluting the clay, and encasing them in a shell of mud.

But their salvation was to come from this hated water.

---

9. The Abbés Le Helloco and Pouchard. We have spoken more than once of the former, a man of great intelligence and of a self-abnegation carried, in the words of Saint Augustine, *usque ad contemptum sui*. His *confrère* was equally devoted.
10. "There is not a single uninjured church in the deanery," declared the Abbé Vanryckeghem, Vicaire of Dixmude. "Nearly forty churches between Nieuport and Ypres have been destroyed."

CHAPTER 8

The Inundation

A new actor was about to appear on the scene, a new ally, slower, but infinitely more effectual, than the best reinforcements.

Last November the *Moniteur Belge* published a royal decree conferring the Order of Leopold upon M. Charles Louis Kogge, *garde wateringue* of the north of Furnes, for his courageous and devoted services in the work of inundation in the Yser region.

It was, we have been told, this M. Kogge who first conceived the idea of calling the waters to our aid. A more romantic version has it that the notion was suggested to the headquarters staff by the singularly opportune discovery of a bundle of old revolutionary documents bearing upon the action brought in 1795 by a Flemish farmer against his landlord "to recover damages for the loss he had suffered through the inundation of his land during the defence of Nieuport." Be this as it may, on the evening of October 25 the Belgian general headquarters staff informed the admiral that it had just taken measures to inundate the left bank of the Yser between that river and the railway line from Dixmude to Nieuport.

The effects of this inundation could not, however, be felt for the first day or two, or even for those immediately following. The word inundation generally suggests to the mind the image of a torrential rush of water, a great charge of marine or fluvial cavalry which sweeps all before it. There was nothing of the sort in this case. We were in Western Belgium, in an invertebrate country, without relief of any sort, where everything proceeds slowly and phlegmatically, even cataclysms. It is, perhaps, a pity that there is not another word in the language to describe the hydrographic operation we were about to witness; but in default of a substantive there is a verb, which surprised most readers of the *communiqués* as a neologism, but which, as a fact, has been used in Flanders from time immemorial, and has the advantage of expressing the nature of the operation most admirably. It is the verb *tendre* (to spread or stretch). They *spread* an inundation there as fishermen spread a net. No image could be more exact. The *spreader*, in this case, was at the locks of Nieuport. He is a head *wateringue*, commanding a dozen men armed with levers to manipulate the lifting-jacks. At high tide he had the flood-gates raised; the sea entered, forcing back the fresh water of the canal and its tributaries; and the sea did not run out again, for the flood-gates had been lowered. Henceforth the fresh water which flowed on every side into the basin of the Yser will find no outlet; "without haste and without rest" it will add its contribution to that of the tide; it will gradually overflow the dykes of the collecting canals, will reach the *watergands*, and cover the whole *schoore* with its meshes. Slyly, noiselessly, unceasingly, it will rise on a soil already saturated like a sponge and incapable of absorbing another drop of water. All that falls there, whether it come from the sky in the form of rain, or from the hills of Cassel in the form of torrents, will remain on the surface. There is no way of checking the inundation as long as the flood-gates are not raised. He who holds Nieuport holds the entire district by means of its locks. This explains the persistence of the Germans in their attempts to capture it. Fortunately, these attempts were somewhat belated; they tried a surprise by the dunes of Lombaertzide and Middelkerke, which might perhaps have succeeded but for the timely co-operation of the Anglo-French fleet with the Belgian troops: the German attack was driven back by the fire of the monitors, and failed to carry the locks of Nieuport. The inundation continued. When its last meshes were woven and all its web complete, it was to spread in a semicircle on a zone of 30 kilometres, and this immense artificial lagoon, from four to five kilometres wide and from three to four feet deep, in which light squadrons and batteries might have engaged if hard pressed, but for the abrupt depressions of the *watergands* and collecting canals, forming invisible traps at every step, was to constitute the most impregnable defensive front, a liquid barrier defying all attacks. Dixmude, at the extremity of this lagoon, in the blind alley here formed by the Yser, the Handzaeme Canal, and the railway embankment, might aptly be compared to Quiberon; like Quiberon, it would be, were its bridges destroyed, a sort of thin, low peninsula; but it is a Flemish Quiberon anchored upon a motionless sea, without waves and without tides, studded with tree-tops and telegraph poles, and bearing on its dead waters the drifting corpses of soldiers and animals, pointed helmets, empty cartridge-cases and food-tins.

CHAPTER 9

The Murder of Commander Jeanniot

On October 25 we had not yet received any help from the inundation. Our troops were in dire need of rest, and the enemy was tightening his grip along the entire front. New reinforcements were coming up to fill the gaps in his ranks; our scouts warned us that fresh troops were marching upon Dixmude by the three roads of Eessen, Beerst, and Woumen.[1] We had to expect a big affair the next day, if not that very night. It came off that night.

About 7 o'clock the Gamas company went to relieve the men in the southern trenches. On their way, immediately outside the town, they fell in with a German force of about the same strength as themselves, which had crept up no one knew how. There was a fusillade and a general *mêlée*, in which our sailors opened a passage through the troop with bayonets and butt-ends, disposing of some forty Germans and putting the rest to flight.[2] Then there was a lull. The splash of rain was the only sound heard till 2 a.m., when suddenly a fresh outbreak of rifle-fire was heard near the Caeskerke station, right inside the defences. It was suggested that our men or our allies, exasperated by their life of continual alarms, had been carried away by some reckless impulse. The bravest soldiers admit that hallucinations are not uncommon at

1. "Germans of the regular army coming from the direction of Reims. The Boches we had had to deal with so far had been volunteers or reservists." (Second-Lieutenant X.'s note-book.)
2. Not without losses on our side. "Saw Gamas, who has had fourteen of his men killed tonight, among them his boatswain Dodu." (Second-Lieutenant Gautier's note-book.)

night in the trenches. All the pitfalls of darkness rise before the mind; the circulation of the blood makes a noise like the tramp of marching troops; if by chance a nervous sentry should fire his rifle, the whole section will follow suit.

Convinced that some misunderstanding of this kind had taken place, the staff, still quartered at the Caeskerke railway station, shouted to the sections to cease firing. As, however, the fusillade continued in the direction of the town, the admiral sent one of his officers, Lieutenant Durand-Gasselin, to reconnoitre. He got as far as the Yser without finding the enemy; the fusillade had ceased; the roads were clear. He set out on his way back to Caeskerke. On the road he passed an ambulance belonging to the brigade going up towards Dixmude, which, on being challenged, replied: "Rouge Croix."[3] Rather surprised at this inversion, he stopped the ambulance; it was full of Germans, who, however, surrendered without offering any resistance. But this capture suggested a new train of thought to the staff: they were now certain that there had been an infantry raid upon the town; the Germans in the ambulance probably belonged to a troop of mysterious assailants who had made their way into Dixmude in the night and had vanished no less mysteriously after this extraordinary deed of daring. One of our covering trenches must have given way, but which? Our allies held the railway line by which the enemy had penetrated into the defences, sounding the charge.... The riddle was very disturbing, but under the veil of a thick damp night, which favoured the enemy, it was useless to seek a solution. It was found next morning at dawn, when one of our detachments on guard by the Yser suddenly noticed in a meadow a curious medley of Belgians, French marines, and Germans. Had our men been made prisoners? This uncertainty was of brief duration. There was a sharp volley; the sailors fell; the Germans made off. This was what had happened:

Various versions have been given of this incident, one of the most dramatic of the defence, in the course of which the heroic Commander Jeanniot and Dr. Duguet, chief officer of the medical staff, fell mortally wounded, with several others. The general opinion, however, seems to be that the German attack, which was delivered at 2.30 a.m., was closely connected with

---

3. *I.e.*, instead of "Croix Rouge," the usual French locution.

the surprise movement attempted at 7 o'clock in the evening on the Eessen road and so happily frustrated by the intervention of the Gamas company. It is not impossible that it was carried out by the fragments of the force we had scattered, reinforced by new elements and charging to the sound of the bugle. This would explain the interval of several hours between the two attacks, which were no doubt the outcome of a single inspiration. An eye-witness says:

> The night was pursuing its normal course, and as there were no indications of disturbance, Dr. Duguet took the opportunity to go and get a little rest in the house where he was living, which was just across the street opposite his ambulance. The Abbé Le Helloco, chaplain of the 2nd Regiment, had joined him at about 1.30 a.m. The latter admits that he was rather uneasy because of the earlier skirmish, in which as was his habit, he had been unremitting in his ministrations to the wounded. After a few minutes' talk the two men separated to seek their straw pallets. The Abbé had been asleep for an hour or two, when he was awakened by shots close at hand. He roused himself and went to Dr. Duguet, who was already up. The two did not exchange a word. Simultaneously, without taking the precaution of extinguishing the lights behind them, they hurried to the street. Enframed by the lighted doorway, they at once became a target; a volley brought them down in a moment. Dr. Duguet had been struck by a bullet in the abdomen; the Abbé was hit in the head, the arm, and the right thigh. The two bodies were touching each other. 'Abbé,' said Dr. Duguet, 'we are done for. Give me absolution. I regret ...' The Abbé found strength to lift his heavy arm and to make the sign of the cross upon his dying comrade. Then he fainted, and this saved him. Neither he nor Dr. Duguet had understood for the moment what was happening. Whence had the band of marauders who had struck them down come, and how had they managed to steal into our lines without being seen? It was a mystery. This fusillade breaking out behind them had caused a certain disorder

in the sections nearest to it, who thought they were being taken in the rear, and who would have been, indeed, had the attack been maintained. The band arrived in front of the ambulance station at the moment when the staff (three Belgian doctors, a few naval hospital orderlies, and Quartermaster Bonnet) were attending to Dr. Duguet, who was still breathing. They made the whole lot prisoners and carried them along in their idiotic rush through the streets. Both officers and soldiers must have been drunk. This is the only reasonable explanation of their mad venture. We held all the approaches to Dixmude; the brief panic that took place in certain sections had been at once controlled. The improbability of a night attack inside the defences was so great that Commander Jeanniot, who had been in reserve that night, and who, roused by the firing like Dr. Duguet and Abbé Le Helloco, had gone into the street to call his sector to arms, had not even taken his revolver in his hand. Mistaking the identity and the intentions of the groups he saw advancing, he ran towards them to reassure them and bring them back to the trenches. This little stout, grizzled officer, rough and simple in manner, was adored by the sailors. He was known to be the bravest of the brave, and he himself was conscious of his power over his men. When he recognised his mistake it was too late. The Germans seized him, disarmed him, and carried him off with loud '*Hochs!*' of satisfaction. The band continued to push on towards the Yser, driving a few fugitives before them, and a part of them succeeded in crossing the river under cover of the general confusion. Happily this did not last long. Captain Marcotte de Sainte-Marie, who was in command of the guard on the bridge, identified the assailants with the help of a searchlight, and at once opened fire upon them.[4] The majority of the Germans within range of our machine-guns were mown down; the rest scattered along the streets and ran to

---

4. We should add, by order of Commander Varney, who, warned by Dr. de Groote, had at once taken the necessary measures. Second-Lieutenant X.'s note-book gives more precise details: "We had succeeded in placing machine-guns on each side of the bridge, which was a revolving bridge, and had just been opened by Commander Varney."

cellars and ruins to hide themselves. But the head of the column had got across with its prisoners, whom they drove before them with the butt-ends of their rifles.[5] For four hours they wandered about, seeking an issue which would enable them to rejoin their lines.

It was raining the whole time. Weary of wading through the mud, the officers stopped behind a hedge to hold a council. A pale light began to pierce the mist; day was dawning, and they could no longer hope to regain the German lines in a body. Prudence dictated that they should disperse until nightfall. But what was to be done with the prisoners? The majority voted that they should be put to death. The Belgian doctors protested. Commander Jeanniot, who took no part in the debate, was talking calmly to Quartermaster Bonnet. At a sign from their leader the Boches knelt and opened fire upon the prisoners. The Commander fell, and as he was still breathing, they finished him off with their bayonets. The only survivors were the Belgian doctors, who had been spared, and Quartermaster Bonnet, who had only been hit in the shoulder. It was at this moment that the marauders were discovered. One section charged them forthwith; another fell back to cut off their retreat. What happened afterwards? Some accounts declare that the German officers learned what it costs to murder prisoners, and that our men despatched the dogs there and then; but the truth is, that, in spite of the general desire to avenge Commander Jeanniot, the whole band was taken prisoner and brought before the admiral, who had only the three most prominent rascals of the gang executed.

---

5. Here there seems to have been some confusion in the eye-witness's account. He leads us to suppose that Dr. Duguet's ambulance was in the town, and that the Germans who killed him and wounded the Abbé Le Helloco went on afterwards to the bridge with their prisoners. "As a fact," we are now told, "the affair took place between the bridge—which the head of a column had crossed by surprise, driving before them a number of Belgians, sailors, and perhaps some marauders—and the level crossing near the station of Caeskerke where the column was finally stopped. It was in this part of the street that Dr. Duguet had his dressing-station; and it was there, too, that Commander Jeanniot, whose reserve post was at Caeskerke, came out to meet the assailants. And it was the fields near the south bank of the Yser to which the column betook itself, dragging its prisoners with it, when it found the road barred." (See M. Thomas Couture's narrative at the end of this chapter.)

Another very interesting account of this episode has been communicated to us by M. Charles Thomas Couture, chauffeur to Commander Varney.

An Unpublished Account of the Murder of Commander Jeanniot

Dixmude, Monday, October 26, 1914

Yesterday we were informed that a certain number of Germans, slipping between the trenches, had managed to get into Dixmude. Search was made in the houses and cellars, and we collected a few prisoners.

This incident caused us some uneasiness, and as the bombardment, which generally ceased at night, continued persistently, I hesitated to go to bed. Shells were bursting quite close to our inn, the front of which was peppered with bullets. Fortunately, the shells were shrapnel, annoying rather than deadly, and as I was very tired, I made up my mind to get a sleep about 10 o'clock. But I lay down fully dressed and armed; I did not even lay aside my revolver.

One after the other the inhabitants of the inn followed my example. There were four of us: Commander Varney, Captain Monnot, Lieutenant Bonneau, and myself. Dr. Duguet and Abbé Le Helloco, who generally shared our straw, were detained at the ambulance by some severe cases, and were not expected to come in before 1 o'clock in the morning. By this time all was quiet, and the bombardment had ceased.

At 3 a.m. a cyclist rushed in, crying: "Get up! The Boches are coming!" I did not for a moment imagine that the enemy had crossed the bridge over the Yser, which was some 80 or 100 metres in front of us. I thought that the Germans had forced the sailors' trenches in front of Dixmude, that they had entered the town in force, and that the line of defence was to be brought back to the canal. If such were the case, it was necessary to get my car ready to start immediately. As soon as I was awake I accordingly went out by the front door of the inn, and going to my car, I began to pump up the petrol. Commander Varney had come out at the same time.

Our common living-room was feebly lighted by a lantern, but this sufficed to throw the figures of those who passed into the embrasure of the door into strong relief. This was the case a few minutes later when Dr. Duguet and Abbé Le Helloco emerged. I was bending down over my car, quite in the dark.

At this moment a body of brawlers passed along the road, coming from the bridge and going towards the level crossing. They were preceded by a bugler, very much out of tune. In spite of the lights and the reports of firearms among the band, I only realised after they had passed that they were the enemy.

But as soon as I grasped the fact I recognised that there was no question of getting out the car just then, so I followed Commander Varney, who was near me. "What shall I do, Commander?" "Above all things, don't let them take you prisoner." Subsequent events made me appreciate the wisdom of this order.

The Commander disappeared in the night, going towards the Yser to see what was happening. I went back into the inn by the back door, and there, stretched on the ground side by side, I found the doctor and the Abbé, on whom the Germans had fired at very short range. Both were wounded in the abdomen. Probably the same bullets went through them both. The doctor murmured: "I am hit in the loins; I can't move my legs." The Abbé seemed to have but one thought: "I won't fall into the hands of the Germans alive." But he managed to give absolution to our poor doctor.

I went out of the inn again, and back to the motors, to see what was happening. I found the cook and the orderlies there; they had taken their rifles and were awaiting events. I joined them, holding my revolver in my hand.

What gave me most anxiety was that not a sound came from the line of the trenches. The rifles were all silent; no night had been so calm. I began to wonder if by some extraordinary surprise all the sailors had been taken prisoners.

As we knew that the enemy troop had passed us and gone

towards the level crossing, we took our stand, in view of their possible return, at the corner of a neighbouring house, where the Belgian soldiers were quartered.

Captain Ferry, who had been wounded a few days before and had his left arm in a sling, joined us.

A suspicious rumbling was heard on the road. Captain Ferry advanced completely out of cover to reconnoitre. He found himself face to face with a band of Germans who barred the road level with the other corner of the Belgians' house.

"Halt!" cried the captain; "you are my prisoners."

"Not at all," replied a voice in guttural French. "It's you who are our prisoners."

This somewhat comic dialogue was not continued, for the sailors Mazet and Pinardeau fired. The Germans never even attempted to retort; they allowed Captain Ferry to re-join us quietly, and disappeared into the ditch by the road.

It was now half-past three. The alarm was over, and had lasted barely half an hour. Our little party took refuge in the cowshed, for the German guns had begun to send us shrapnel shells, which exploded high in the air, but nevertheless covered us with fragments. All we could do was to wait for the day, which at this date broke about half-past four. Lieutenant Bonneau had brought a half-section of sailors to our inn, and these began to explore the neighbourhood.

Some Belgian soldiers joined the sailors, and a *battue* of Boches began in the marshy meadows. We heard cries of "There they are! There they are!" and shots were fired; then "Don't fire, they are sailors." Presently it was all over, and prisoners passed on their way to the admiral, who was installed at the level crossing.

We then heard that nothing at all had happened in the trenches. The troop that had attacked us was composed of Boches who had managed to creep into the town secretly. Led by one or two officers, they had crossed the bridge over the canal, killing the sentries, seriously wounding Lieutenant de Lambertye, and then pushing forward. As they passed they went into the houses that showed lights, notably that occupied by the staff of the 1st Regiment, where they killed two cooks and wounded a chauffeur. As we have seen, they then shot our doctor and our chaplain, and their military operations ended herewith, for their subsequent deeds were murder pure and simple.

I was told the story at dawn, when I found myself face to face with Quartermaster Bonnet, chauffeur to the adjutant-major, who, to my great surprise, had his right arm in a sling. "Well, M. Couture," he said, "I shan't be able to drive Captain Monnot any more." I questioned him, and he then told me that he, assisted by some Belgian orderlies and doctors, had gone out to take Dr. Duguet to the ambulance. Suddenly the party found themselves face to face with the German troop, which was returning. The Boches seized the stretcher-bearers, and the doctor was left by the side of the ditch. Perhaps he was finished off there.

The Germans had several other prisoners, notably Commander Jeanniot. This remarkable man, who was no less beloved than esteemed, was with the first battalion, which he commanded, in reserve some distance to the rear. The noise and the shots awoke him, and he came out alone upon the road to see what was happening. The Germans crouching in the ditches had no difficulty in seizing him, and his five stripes made them realise the importance of their capture.

In all there were some dozen prisoners, whom the Germans carried along with them across the fields, and whom they did not scruple to put in front of them during the firing. This explains the hesitation shown during the chase. Seeing that they were caught, the German officers were not long in making up their minds. "Shoot the prisoners!" It must be noted that there was a certain reluctance in the German ranks, perhaps even a certain opposition to this barbarous order. We learned later that the recalcitrants were Berlin students who had volunteered for service. Was this a movement of humanity or merely a measure of precaution taken with a view to their own fate?

However, there are always some ready to carry out brutal orders. The Mausers were fired at the heads of the prisoners. Commander Jeanniot was struck by several bullets, the whole of the front of his skull being blown off. Several of the Belgians fell. My comrade Bonnet, if I understood him aright, made the movement of a child who dodges a box on the ear. That saved him; the bullet aimed at his head went into his right shoulder. At this moment he saw our sailors and the Belgians coming up, and running as fast as he could lay legs to the ground, he called to them: "Go at them; there are only about forty of them left." The rest had made off across the fields.

At 7 a.m. they were all prisoners.

The admiral at once decided that the murderers should be shot there and then. But as Frenchmen are not given to wholesale executions, the prisoners who had been rescued were called upon to point out the ringleaders.

A few seconds later four volleys told me that military justice had taken its rapid course.

Almost at the same moment the body of Commander Jeanniot was carried in. His cyclists and his chauffeur would not allow anyone but themselves to render him this last service. They carried their chief on a stretcher borne on their shoulders, and all had tears in their eyes.

The rest of the morning was quiet. A German effort was being made further to the north, where we heard furious fighting.

As we were drinking our coffee the Senegalese riflemen arrived to support the sailors. They were received with joy, for the brigade was much exhausted.

CHAPTER 10

In the Trenches

Thus ended this dramatic episode, of which neither the genesis nor the results have been fully elucidated so far. Did the German troop which overran the town during the night, and of which only a portion got away to the meadows with the prisoners, consist of a battalion or a half-battalion? The fire of Captain Marcotte de Sainte-Marie's guns had laid a good many of the enemy low. "We were walking over their corpses in the street," wrote Marine H. G.[1] The next day we turned a fair number of the assailants out of the cellars where they had hidden. But the majority, aided by mysterious accomplices, certainly managed to escape.

In any case, the surprise had been a sharp lesson, showing us how necessary it was that our positions should be immediately reinforced. The admiral represented this to headquarters, and two battalions of Senegalese were despatched from Loo. Meanwhile the bombardment had been resumed. It became very intense between eleven and three o'clock, and was directed mainly to the bridges of Dixmude and the trenches in the cemetery. We had some heavy casualties there, notably Lieutenant Eno[2] and part of the seventh company of the second battalion. But the morale of the men was

---

1. "Blood ran in the streets like water," said Jean Claudius still more emphatically, according to a witness. This was probably the origin of the fantastic accounts which appeared in the press at this period, most of them purely imaginary.

---

2. We must quote this short passage from the eloquent speech made at the funeral of this brave officer at Lannion by Second-Lieutenant de Cuverville, representing Admiral Berryer: "The order to mobilise found Ernest Eno at Brest, engaged in training those very battalions he was later to lead against the enemy; and no one could have been better qualified than he to give our young recruits not only professional instruction, but those lessons of (continued on next page)

perfectly maintained. We may cite the case of Quartermaster Leborgne, wounded in the head and taken to the dressing-station during a lull in the fighting, who escaped when he heard the cannonade resumed and came back to die at his post, or the bugler Chaupin, who, seeing the recruits arching their backs under the hail of bullets, cried, "Look at me, little ones," and drawing himself up to his full height with magnificent bravery, crossed the danger zone, carrying his comrades along in the wake of his heroism.[3] Thanks to the reconnaissances of his airmen and the spies he had in the town, the enemy's fire was surprisingly accurate. One of the officers who commanded a much-exposed section, Second-Lieutenant T. S., wrote:

> In the space of two hours, from half-past ten to half-past twelve in the morning, some fifty shrapnel shells fell round us. At one o'clock a quarter of my men were out of action. I asked for reinforcements and provisions; we had been in the firing line for sixty hours. The Commander gave me a verbal order to fall back. I consulted my petty officers and my men. 'Shall we fall back without being relieved?' 'We can't do it, lieutenant.' An hour later I received a written order to abandon the trench. I had to obey, after we had buried our dead and carried off our wounded. You see, dear parents, what our sailors will do: they will hold out to the last gasp. That same evening the trench was occupied by another section of the brigade.

And that same evening of October 26 this trench—or another—was again attacked, and was only saved for us by a prodigy of heroism. The enemy had advanced to within a few yards, and charged, shouting "Hurrah!" Our machine-guns were very dirty

---

manliness and patriotism which go to the heart, and make men strong and courageous. For he was himself a hero. A self-made man, he had raised himself step by step on the steep ladder of his calling. He was a true sailor. He went off with the 1st Regiment of marines on August 13.... He fell at the head of his men under intense fire round the cemetery of Dixmude, his thigh fractured by a fragment of shell. He was not fated to recover from his terrible wound. He died, uniting in his last prayers to God his dear ones and his beloved Brittany, which he was to see no more." An operation had been performed on Eno on the battlefield by his fellow-citizen and friend Dr. Taburet, one of the doctors of the brigade, who showed the most supreme contempt of danger under fire in attendance on our wounded.
3. Dr. Caradec, *op. cit.*

and would not work.[4] But Lieutenant Martin des Pallières was in command of the section. It was holding the road to Woumen, between the wall of the cemetery and a trench dug on the other side in a beetroot field. Des Pallières sprang upon the parapet.

"Boys," he cried, "we must receive these gentry with cold steel. Fix bayonets!"

And when one of the marines, a Parisian, who had charged too vigorously, lamented the loss of his "hat-pin" (his bayonet), which he had left in a German hide, Des Pallières replied: "Do as I do; charge with your head."[5] The next day he was killed by a shell.

---

4. In less critical circumstances the same accident had happened to Second-Lieutenant Gautier, and was the occasion of an amusing little scene, which might have been taken from Léonec and Gervèze's sketches of marines: "Yesterday I was going at the Germans with machine-guns at 1,200 metres on a road from which I finally cut them off. All of a sudden the guns jammed. I yelled from my blockhouse: 'What's the matter?' 'Guns jammed.' 'Tell the gunner from me that he's an ass.' The communicator, a worthy Breton fisherman, repeated gravely: 'The lieutenant says that the gunner is an ass.' The gunner was one Primat. A few days later, on November 10, in submerged Dixmude, this same Primat (the orderly of the second-lieutenant), who had survived his officer, used his machine-guns with such skill and coolness against a German column that he stopped it dead, mowing down three sections."

5. This story is told by the Marine Georges Delaballe. Such was the ardour communicated by Des Pallières to his men, that the next day a marine and a Boche were found "lying dead one upon the other, the marine's fingers thrust through the German's cheek, and still clutching it." A stray bullet had killed them both. What had exasperated the marines was that the major who led the attack wore a large Red Cross armlet. Their native honesty was revolted by this constant recourse to ignoble ruses, by which our enemies have dishonoured even their own heroism. Martin des Pallières was the nephew of the admiral who commanded the marines in 1870. "He was a brave man, whose courage was combined with great simplicity and gaiety. He was killed by a big shell in the middle of the group of machine-guns he was working under a furious fire," writes a correspondent. Dr. Caradec points out that this night of October 26 was particularly tragic; and in support of this statement he quotes an incident horrible enough, indeed, from the narrative of the naval mechanician Le L.: "The Germans had taken some French trenches, and shells were raining thickly upon us. All of a sudden some of our men were engulfed in a mass of debris. As one of my friends was half buried in the earth, I and another went to help him; but a shell fell right upon him, and I in my turn was buried up to the neck. Night was coming on fast. I spent fourteen hours of anguish in this position. Furious fighting was going on. Two friends were moaning near me. The one nearest begged me to help him, but I was held fast as in a vice, and had to look on helpless as he died. My own strength began to fail. I became unconscious a few hours after I had been buried. What made me suffer most was to see the Germans a few yards from me. I could see all they were doing, all their death-dealing preparations.

Meanwhile the brigade had passed under the command of General Grossetti, who had undertaken the defence of the line of the Yser as far as, and inclusive of, Dixmude (detachment of the army of Belgium under General d'Urbal). The day of the 27th passed without an attack in force; the enemy merely bombarded us. He gave us time to breathe the following night and morning till 9 a.m. Then the hurly-burly began again. An officer of the Naval Reserve who received his baptism of fire that day, Lieutenant Alfred de la Barre de Nanteuil, grandson of General Le Flô, wrote to his family that he had been specially favoured.

It was a fine christening, plenty of sweetmeats, the whole show, bullets, shrapnel, and, above all, the famous 'saucepans' (*marmites*). Chance treated me well.

In his section alone there were four killed, twelve wounded, and eleven missing. This was the prelude to a sudden attack, directed against the trenches in the cemetery, to which the enemy paid particular attention. But we knew this, and had put our steadiest troops there. The attack was again repulsed, thanks mainly to the firmness of the first musketry instructor, Le Breton, who had already been wounded on the 24th, and who took command of the company when all the officers had been put out of action.[6]

During the night the Senegalese riflemen retook our lost trenches; they set to work to clear away the rubbish and found my two dead friends near me. One of the Senegalese stepped on my head. Feeling something under his feet, he bent down and saw me. They got me out and took me to the first ambulance. In a few hours I was fully conscious again. You can imagine how I rejoiced to find myself among friends. I felt like one risen from the dead."

6. Among them was Second-Lieutenant Gautier. The following order, communicated to us by his family, was found with his papers: "Monsieur Gautier,—By superior orders, I am sending a section to relieve you, and to instruct you to go with your section near the cemetery, behind the wall or on the railway embankment, as may seem best to you and to the officer in the adjoining trenches. Des Pallières' section, which was in the cemetery, has been annihilated, Des Pallières himself killed and buried in the debris of the trench." Second-Lieutenant Gautier was killed at 9 o'clock in the evening. "We were having our dinner in the trench," wrote Lieutenant Gamas a few days later, "when the order came for him to go to a dangerous position to replace Des Pallières, who had just been killed there. The last words your son-in-law said to me were: 'Captain, it's my turn.' We shook hands warmly, looking affectionately at each other. The next day I heard that my poor friend was dead. He had been hit in the forehead by a German bullet at the moment when, attacked by very superior numbers with three machine-gun sections, he had put his head out in order to regulate his fire and do his duty thoroughly. He fell nobly, leaving a glorious and honoured name to his wife and children."

Our allies were less fortunate on the line from Dixmude to Nieuport, where the 4th Belgian Division, overwhelmed by superior numbers, had to fall back beyond Ramscappelle and Pervyse. The strategic importance of these two villages made it imperative to retake them immediately. Every available man was sent from the brigade on the evening of the 29th. This did not prevent the enemy from continuing his bombardment of Dixmude, to which this time we were able to reply very efficaciously with our heavy artillery. This secured us a fairly quiet night. Such nights were few and far between in the brigade. "We don't know what it is to sleep," wrote a sailor. "We haven't closed our eyes for ten days." Perhaps the enemy was as weary as our men. His sole manifestation that night was to send a few shrapnel shells upon Caeskerke and the cross-roads where the admiral had taken up his position. Perhaps, too, he was less interested in Dixmude than in Ramscappelle and Pervyse at this stage of the operations. At dawn he rushed Ramscappelle, but he was repulsed at Pervyse, which the two companies of Rabot's battalion defended with their accustomed vigour. The night before, however, the railway bridge of Dixmude had been demolished by a big shell.

In the brief intervals of this exhausting struggle, the eyes of the defenders were turned inquiringly on the *schoore* of the Yser. How slowly the inundation announced by the Belgian headquarters staff on the 25th seemed to be spreading! The progress it had made in five days was almost imperceptible. And yet surely it was advancing now on the great level plain; the *watergands* were overflowing; the meshes of the watery net were drawing together and encircling villages and farms. Near Ramscappelle and Pervyse it had already formed a large continuous expanse.

That day the first tactical effects of the inundation made themselves felt on our north. Ramscappelle had been retaken by the 42nd Division in a brilliant bayonet charge; the enemy had been driven back behind the embankment of the Dixmude-Nieuport railway, whence he had almost immediately retired upon the Yser: he was falling back not only before our troops, but before the insidious rising of the waters. The plan of the German general staff was foiled. In their attempt upon Dunkirk they had not reckoned upon the intervention of the Anglo-French fleet, which prevented them from making their way along the dunes of the seashore, nor upon the advantages offered to the defence by the inundation of the basin of the Yser. The key of the position was neither at Dixmude, Pervyse, Ramscappelle, nor Ypres, as they had supposed, but in the pocket of the head *wateringue* in charge of the locks at Nieuport.

At this moment of the crisis a certain vacillation seemed to prevail in the councils of the enemy. The German staff, though they had not forgotten Dixmude, were apparently casting their eyes in other directions. On the 30th and 31st they barely sent their daily ration of shrapnel and big shells to our trenches in the cemetery and the houses near the bridge. It had been raining incessantly for three days; our men were standing half-way up their legs in water in the trenches. What had become of the spruce "young ladies with the red pompons" of the early days? "You should see us walk," wrote a sailor, one L., of Audierne. "We are like old fellows of seventy. I have no feeling in my poor knees and elbows." But the most severe suffering was caused by want of socks; the men could hardly stand on their naked feet, purple with cold, in their hard boots. "This is the campaign of frozen toes," says one of the sufferers. Inured to discipline and naturally fatalistic, they did not complain, and looked to their families to help them in their trouble. "Do send me some socks. I have to go barefoot, and it is very cold," wrote one sailor, J. F., of Le Passage Lauriec; and in his next letter he repeats:

I can tell you, my dear parents, that the weather is very bad here, rain and wind every day, and the cold! Sleeping in the trenches is not very easy. I have not closed my eyes for a fortnight, what with the cold and the shells and bullets. Still I keep a good heart. My feet are bare in my shoes, and they are always icy cold. If you send me some socks, will you put some tobacco in with them?

Another letter is in the same strain:

Dear mother,
You say my brother is still drinking, and this is very wrong of him, but that he took the socks off his own feet to send them to me. I thank him very much, for I did want them badly.

The Breton drunkard can be generous!

There were lucky ones here as elsewhere. Such was H. L., who made himself some mittens with a pair of old socks found in a German trench. Men are not very squeamish in war-time, when they have been wearing the same ragged filthy garments for a month. "You could not touch my vest with a pair of tongs, it is so dirty," wrote the same H. L. to his sister. The officers were no better off, except that they had socks. Alfred de Nanteuil wrote:

We never change; we never wash; we never brush our hair. I have been living in the same grime ever since I left Brest. The only things I have changed are my socks. All my ideas of hygiene are upset, for, on the whole, I have never felt so well.

Some few complain of the food. "I have been three days in the trenches without enough to eat," grumbles one sailor J. L. R. But the majority declare that the tinned meat was not bad, especially when it was warmed, and that, on the whole, they got enough.[7] As for drink, with the exception of the coffee, pronounced "famous," the unanimous verdict was that it was execrable, neither wine nor beer, only stagnant water; "and they say, besides, that the Boches have poisoned it." The men were recommended only to drink it in their coffee, well boiled. "I lived for days on bread and sugar, with a cup of coffee for an occasional treat," wrote Alfred de Nanteuil. "All the water in the district is polluted. So I go very well for a week without drinking anything but coffee." François Alain, for one, was four days without food or drink, lying among the straw in a barn where twenty-seven of his comrades had been bayoneted. How did this nineteen-year-old conscript escape the Boches who had remained in the neighbourhood? Through a little hole he had made with his knife in one of the tiles of the roof he observed all their movements, and took note of their trenches and the emplacements of their cannon and their machine-guns; and one fine night, when there was not too much moonlight, he crawled out, killing a German officer who was reconnoitring the French positions, and got back into our lines with a cargo of precious information, a thick coating of mud, and teeth sharpened

---

7. All the officers we have seen or who have written to us declare that the transport service was excellent throughout the defence, in spite of the greatest difficulties, and that the naval commissariat was irreproachable.

by a fast of ninety-six hours.[8] And these men, dripping with wet, with empty stomachs and burning heads, never lost heart for a moment. The same note recurs in all their letters: "In spite of this, all goes well, and we are not downhearted, especially when we can have a go at the Boches." The one thing consoles them for the other. They know the perils of the trenches, and they prefer them to the inactivity of being kept in reserve. "We have had twelve days of fighting now," wrote the Marine C., of Audierne, "and this evening, I am glad to say, we are to be in the first line, for it is better to be under fire than resting." Was this paradox or braggadocio? Not at all. They spoke as they thought. They courted danger as other men shun it.

---

8. He was decorated with the military medal by General Foch in person.

CHAPTER 11

The Attack on the
Château De Woumen

All Saints' Day was nearly as quiet as the preceding forty-eight hours. We re-established our trenches, and the admiral reorganised his regiments and transferred his headquarters to Oudecappelle. In his journal Alfred de Nanteuil, who had been with our second line from the day before, notices the truce from *marmites*, if not from shrapnel and bullets, "singing past a little like summer flies." But farms were blazing all round the vast horizon, lighting up the November night and accentuating the fact that, although the enemy's attentions had changed in form, they had put on no amenity. "One of my men," says De Nanteuil, "found the severed hand of a small child in a German's knapsack...." And at Eessen, where the *vicaire* was a young priest of twenty-eight, the Abbé Deman, his murderers amused themselves by forcing him to dig his own grave before they shot him in the graveyard of his own church.[1]

A day later the temporary inertia of the enemy was explained. A few *marmites* on our trenches and on the farms occupied by our supply services were not enough to deceive us. We had been aware for several days of a continuous growling in the south-west, on the Ypres road. The enemy had transferred a part of his forces towards Mercken, where he was seeking contact with our Territorials and with the British troops. It seemed a good opportunity to break the iron girdle which held us and to afford some relief to our positions. The morale of our men had never been better. Rumours

---

1. Declaration of the Abbé Vanryckeghem, who affirms that the *curés* of Saint Georges, of Mannekensverke, and of Vladsloo were also executed.

of a general offensive were current in the brigade, and nothing stimulates the French soldier more than the hope of an advance. On November 3 French aeroplanes passed over Dixmude, towards the German lines, and a balloon was hanging in the sky towards the west. De Nanteuil wrote:

> Happy omen! We have been without such encouragements all through the long defence.... Now my spirits rise. Everything points to an advance. The *marmites* have disappeared, for which no one is sorry. I have been in the first line since last night. The sun is shining; the lark is singing; the mud is drying. We are fearful to behold. Relieved by the Belgians in the night, I have to find and guide those who have to take the place of my company. On my way back, worn out, I stop a barrel of Belgian soup and have a delicious pull at it. My battalion is in reserve since last night. Passed the night in a barn, men in the trench. Today it has been a case of 'packs on' ever since the morning.

Where are we off to? said this intrepid officer to himself. *Perhaps,* he thought, *nowhere!* Anyway, the guns are raging, and this time it is our own beloved guns, which we have awaited so impatiently. I cannot hear the others; I think it is all right. Alfred de Nanteuil was not mistaken. This time it was our 75s which led the dance. The general had decided that an attack should debouch from the town. . .

> . . . supported by a powerful mass of artillery and having for main objective the *château* on the road to Woumen, about a kilometre from Dixmude.

The attack was to be made by four battalions of infantry of the 42nd Division, a marine battalion under Commandant de Jonquières acting as support, and the rest of the brigade as reserve. The whole was under the command of General Grossetti—Grossetti the invulnerable, as he had been called ever since his splendid defence of Pervyse, where he faced the shells sitting on a camp-stool.

The attack began about eight o'clock by an energetic clearing of the whole position. There was, perhaps, some little hesitation in the movements which followed. The fact is that by not moving off until half-past eleven in the morning our infantry lost much of the advantage given by the artillery preparation. The enemy had had time to pull himself together. The eighth battalion of Chasseurs could not debouch from the cemetery by the Woumen road until supported by the De Jonquières battalion. Then it was checked at the end of 200 metres. At the same time the 151st Infantry had made good a similar advance on the Eessen road. That was the total gain of the day. We renewed the offensive at 3 next morning, but with no more success than the day before. The attack always lacked "go." We scarcely advanced at all, well supported as we were by our 75s, which once more showed their superiority over the German artillery. The general now determined to reinforce the attack with the whole 42nd Division and two fresh battalions of marines. A day was taken up by preparations for the passage of the Yser, a kilometre below Dixmude. For this purpose two flying bridges were brought down from the town. There was a thick fog, the best sort of weather for such an operation. One of the marine battalions was directed to attack on a line parallel to the Yser. The remaining two, crossing higher up, were to make straight for the Château, while the 8th Chasseurs were to prolong the attack to the north. Fifty guns concentrated their fire on the buildings and the ground immediately about them. But this enchanted castle, with its fougasses, its deep trenches, its lines of barbed wire, its loopholed walls, its machine-guns on every storey, and its flanking fire, gave out a sort of repelling electricity which had the effect, if not of destroying the *élan* of our troops, at least of curiously blunting it. The ground, seamed with watercourses, was unfavourable, and trouble brooded in the fog. In short, when night fell we were still a quarter of a mile from the *château*; we had not even reached the park. On the Eessen side we had made no progress. Finally, the Belgians near Beerst, who were defending the north front of Dixmude, sent word that they were no longer enough to man the trenches, and the admiral had to send to their help two companies of the De Kerros battalion from the first reserve. This unwelcome necessity was made up for by the arrival of two long 120-mm. pieces, which were at once put in battery south of the level crossing at Caeskerke.

However, the night of November 5 was quiet all round Dixmude; but at dawn the attack was renewed. This time we had good reason to hope for success. Rising from the provisional trenches, our battalions moved simultaneously in echelon across the plain. The

The "Kiekenstraat" (Chicken Street) after the first days of the bombardment

charge sounded, shouts of "Vive la France!" broke out, and, in spite of terrible machine-gun and rifle fire, the farm and the park were carried with a rush. Our men were at the foot of the *château*. But there the rush was stopped. Contrary to report, the *château* was not taken. The internal defences had been organised in the most formidable way, perhaps even before the war began. The enemy left in our hands some hundred prisoners, who had been barricaded in the pavilion at the main gate.[2] At nightfall the order was given to retire. The De Jonquières battalion returned to its billets. The 42nd Division went off in another direction,[3] and the brigade was again left alone at Dixmude with a handful of Senegalese and the Belgians.[4]

De Nanteuil writes on November 6:

> We don't budge. Our reinforcements are being sent back. Visited the church and Hôtel de Ville of Dixmude. Frightful! They are nothing but shapeless ruins. There is not a whole house left. Certain quarters are destroyed down to their very foundations; they are nothing but heaps of stone and bricks.... Messina is in better case than this unhappy town.

---

2. This, however, is not certainly established. For this account of the closing scenes of the attack we have followed the narrative of the correspondent of *La Liberté*, which appeared to us trustworthy. This correspondent says: "They (the prisoners) had no time to retreat, so sudden and furious was the attack. Carried away by their excitement, the marines never saw that the pavilion was full of Germans. It was not until three hours later that a Prussian non-commissioned officer walked unarmed out of the building and surrendered with his party to the first French officer he met. We have been authoritatively told that nothing of the kind took place. 'The attack reached the Château, but failed to carry it.'"

3. At Dixmude the 4th and 5th had passed in comparative tranquillity. "It rains," writes Alfred de Nanteuil on the 4th, "five hours drawn up on the road, fully accoutred. Mud frightful. Walked through Dixmude—a vision of horror, lights of pillagers, carcases, indescribable ruins.... Passed the night at a deserted farm, full of corpses, utterly sacked and ruined. Plenty of evidence that the owners were well-behaved, pious, and honest Belgian cultivators. The night fairly calm, so we had six hours of sleep in our wet clothes. Impossible to change." The 5th: "Today the weather beautiful, the sun shining. Everything calm. In the watercourses we see reflected the vaporous landscapes of the great Flemish masters. The cattle which have escaped the bombardment stand about on the dykes. At last one is able to breathe, ... to be glad one lives. I begin to think we shall be here for a long time."

4. It came at this juncture under the command of General Bidon. Shortly before it had received an interesting visit. On November 2 a naval lieutenant, De Perrinelle, writes in his diary that Colonel Seely, sometime Minister of War in England, had visited this front and had told them that they had saved the situation by their vigorous resistance.

CHAPTER 12

The Death of Dixmude

She is not quite dead yet, however. Scalped, shattered, and burnt as she is, she still holds a spark of life as long as we are there. This charnel-house in which we are encamped, with its streets, which are nothing but malodorous paths winding among corpses, heaps of broken stone and brick, and craters opened by the Boche *marmites*, still beats with life in its depths. Existence has become subterranean. Dixmude has catacombs into which our men pour when they leave the trenches. And they are not all soldiers who explore the recesses of these vaults and cellars. The suspicious lights alluded to by Alfred de Nanteuil are not, perhaps, always carried by pillagers. Mysteriously enough, one house in the town has escaped the bombardment. It is the flour factory near the bridge, and its cement platform still dominates the valley of the Yser.

The 42nd Division left us two of its batteries of 75s when it moved off. That was something, of course, though not enough to make up for the disablement of 58 out of the 72 guns we originally had for the defence of our front. The only formidable guns we have are the heavy ones, but they are without the mobility of the 75s. And now apparently our attack on the *château* of Woumen has disquieted the Germans, who are again in force before Dixmude. The bombardment of the town and of the trenches has recommenced, and last night we had to repulse a pretty lively attack on our trenches at the cemetery. There is also pressure along the Eessen road, with considerable losses at both points. A renewal of the attack tonight seems probable. And our ranks are already thin![1]

1. For the period between October 24 and November 6 the names of the following officers who fell must be added to those already (continued on next page)

A marine from Dixmude writes on November 7:

Mother, it is with my cartridge belt on my back and sheltered from the German machine-guns that I send you these few lines to say that my news is good, and that I hope it is the same with you and the family. But, mother, I don't expect that either you or the family will ever see me again. None of us will come back. But I shall have given my life in doing my duty as a French soldier-sailor. I have already had two bullets, one in the sleeve of my great-coat, the other in my right cartridge case. The third will do better.

On the same day another marine writes home: "Out of our squad of 16, we still have three left." However, the night of the 6th and the day which followed were quiet enough. The disappointment caused by the failure of our attack on the *château* was already almost forgotten, and our hopes were again rising.

"I think," wrote Alfred de Nanteuil, "that my company will not stir from this for some time. I have to furnish reinforcing parties as they are wanted, the rest of my men and myself staying in the trench, which we are always improving. We have a farmhouse near by which allows us to eat in comfort. And we have plenty of straw."

The general impression is that we are held from one end of the front to the other. "Bombardment always and musketry, a siege war, in short. It will come to an end some day. Meanwhile," says De Nanteuil, gaily, "our spirits and health are good." But this very afternoon certain suspicious movements were descried on the further bank of the Yser. As it was easy to bombard this part of the hostile front, a gun was promptly trained in that direction. Was it a decoy, or was some spy from behind sending signals? The gun no sooner came into action than a German battery was unmasked upon it, killing Captain Marcotte de Sainte-Marie, who was controlling the fire.[2]

---

given: killed or dead of their wounds, Lieutenants Cherdel and Richard, Second-Lieutenants Rousset and Le Coq; among those wounded, but not mortally, Lieutenants Antoine, "son of Admiral Antoine and the model of a perfect officer" (private correspondence), and Revel, who, when severely wounded in the thigh, ordered his decimated company to retire, "leaving him in the trench where he had fallen."
2. Marcotte de Sainte-Marie was provisionally succeeded at the head of his battalion by Lieutenant Dordet, who acquitted himself admirably.

Thenceforward attacks never ceased. The night between the 7th and 8th was nothing but a long series of attempts on our front, which were all repulsed. They began again at daylight against the trenches at the cemetery. There the enclosing wall had been battered down for some time past by the German artillery. Through the loopholes in our parapets one could see the wide stretch of beetroots on the edge of which we were fighting, our backs to Dixmude. Away on the horizon the *château* of Woumen, on its solitary height, rose from the surrounding woods and dominated the position. Little clouds of white smoke hung from the trees, which seemed to be shedding down. In his invariable fashion, the enemy was preparing his attacks by a systematic clearing of the ground; shrapnel and *marmites* were smashing the tombstones, decapitating the crosses, breaking up the iron grilles, the crowns of *immortelles*, and the coffins themselves. The Flemish subsoil is so permeable that coffins are not sunk more than a couple of feet below the surface, so that their occupants were strewn about in a frightful way. Several marines were wounded by splinters of bone from these mobilised corpses.... In the fogs of Flanders, when the mystery of night and the great disc of the moon added their phantasmagoria to the scene, all this surpassed in macabre horror the most ghastly inventions of romantic fiction and legend. Familiar as our Bretons were with supernatural ideas, they shivered at it all, and welcomed an attack as a relief from continual nightmare.[3]

A marine writes:

Although we did not give way at all we understood that everyone was not made like ourselves and the Senegalese. We took pity on the poor worn-out Belgians, who had come to the end of their tether, especially their foot Chasseurs,[4] and we took their places in the trenches. We had three *aviatiks*

---

3. And yet these cemetery trenches afforded comparative security. Before reaching them it was necessary to cross a perfectly flat zone of 60 metres, continually swept by rifle fire and shrapnel. "This we passed at the double, in Indian file, our knapsacks on our heads, and popped, those who had not been left on the way, into the cellars under the caretaker's house with an '*Ouf!*' of relief." (Georges Delaballe.)

4. It must be remembered that the Belgians had been fighting for three solid months, and that until the 23rd October they had faced the Germans alone, if not at Dixmude at least as far north as Nieuport.

continually hanging over us,[5] at which we fired in vain. They returned every day at the same hour, as surely as poverty to the world. As soon as they had gone back we knew what to expect. Down came the *marmites* on our devoted heads!

And their music, compared to the gentle coughing of our little Belgian guns! At last a dozen new 75s appeared on the scene and relieved these poor asthmatics. They were distributed between Caeskerke and the Yser. Our grim point was the cemetery. There one of our trenches had been taken by the Germans, but a vigorous counter-attack, led by Second-Lieutenant Melchior, soon turned them out. "Exasperated by so many sterile efforts," writes Lieutenant A., "the enemy decided, on November 10, to make a decisive stroke. Towards ten in the morning began the most terrible bombardment the brigade had yet had to suffer. The fire was very accurate, destroying the trenches and causing great losses."[6] At 11 o'clock 12,000 Germans, Mausers at the charge, advanced against Dixmude.[7]

This attack repeated the tactics of the early days of the siege. The Germans came on in heavy masses, reinforced by fresh troops. They had also learnt the weak points of their opponents. And yet it is not certain that the attack would have succeeded had it not been for the unexpected giving way of our positions on the Eessen road.[8] This was the only part of the southern sector not defended by marines. It must have been entirely smashed up, with the Senegalese who flanked it on both wings. As a fact, the

---

5. To say nothing of a captive balloon. "Violent bombardment of our trenches, directed by 'sausage' balloons; feeble reply of French and Belgian artillery," is the entry, under date of the 8th, in an officer's note-book, where also we find under date of the 9th: "Bombardment continued. Night attack on the outposts, which were driven in."
6. Dr. Caradec says the German artillery, consisting of batteries of 105s and 77s, was posted 2,000 metres away, behind the Château of Woumen, and near Vladsloo, Kortec-keer, and Kasterthoeck.
7. Before that, however, at half-past nine, a lively attack had been directed against the front of the ninth and tenth companies of the 1st Regiment, which occupied towards Beerst one end of the arc described round Dixmude by our trenches; the extremities of this arc rested on the Yser. The Germans tried to push between the Yser and the flank of the ninth company. This attack was repulsed by the two companies, assisted by fire from the remaining trenches and a battery of 75s.
8. Rather above Dixmude station, between the railway embankment and the Eessen road.

Old houses on the Handzaeme Canal

enemy's fire was so intense along the whole line and our reply so feeble, that Alfred de Nanteuil, who occupied a trench in rear of the northern sector, had to withdraw his men behind a haystack. "Impossible to lift one's nose above the ground," writes an officer, "so thick and fast came the shells." The attacking column was thus enabled to pass the canal at Handzaeme and to fall upon the flank of the trenches occupied by the eleventh company. This company had been engaging the batteries at Korteckeer and Kasterthoeck, on their left, and a violent rifle and machine-gun fire from a group of farms higher up the canal. What was left of it had barely time to fall back upon its neighbours, the ninth and tenth companies. A hostile detachment, creeping along the canal, had contrived to push as far as the command post of the third battalion, taking possession on the way of Dr. Guillet's ambulance, which had been established at the end of the Roman bridge. Our trenches were not connected by telephone, and communications had broken down. Four marines only, out of the 60 in the reserve of Commander Rabot, succeeded in escaping. The sentry on the roof of the farm in which they were waiting saw the enemy coming and gave the alarm: "The Boches—quarter of a mile away!" "To arms!" shouted De Nanteuil. "Into the trenches!"

He himself went to an exposed point to observe the enemy. There a bullet hit him in the neck, striking the spinal marrow. How his men contrived to bring him off it is difficult to say. He remained conscious and had no illusions as to his state. All his energy seemed concentrated on the desire to die in France. He had his wish.[9]

9. We find in the *Bulletin de la Société Archéologique du Finisterre* that "M. de Nanteuil, a retired naval officer, returned to the service in the first days of the war and was attached to the defence of Brest and its neighbourhood. But this occupation seemed to him too quiet, and, in spite of a precarious state of health, he left no stone unturned to get to the front. Fifteen days after arriving there he was killed, one hero more in a family of heroes. He was an efficient archaeologist, especially in all that had to do with military architecture. He had published some excellent papers on our old feudal castles in the *Bulletins* of the *Association Bretonne*, historical notes and descriptions relating to the Château of Brest, the remains at Morlaix and Saint Pol de Léon, the churches of Guimilian, Lampaul, Saint Thégonnec, and Pleyben...." He went off full of pluck and go, we hear from another source, his heart full of eagerness to meet the enemy. Those friends who saw him off all noticed his radiant looks.... When mortally wounded, for paralysis supervened almost at once, and carried to the ambulance, his head was still clear, he was anxious as to the phases of the battle, and asked whether the enemy had been (continued on next page)

Then came the final defeat. The lines on the Eessen road driven in, the dyke pierced at the centre, the northern sector cut off from the south, the German wave flowed over us. The enemy had penetrated to the heart of our defence, and, being continuously reinforced, swept round our flanks and took us in reverse. One after another our positions gave way. Already the first fugitives were arriving before Dixmude.

"Where are you off to?" cries an officer as he bars the way to a sailor.

"Captain, a shell has smashed my rifle. Give me another, and I'll go back."

They give him one, and he returns to the inferno. Another, wandering on the field like a soul in torture, replies to the inquiry of an officer that he is "looking for his company. There cannot be much of it left, but," straightening himself, "that does not matter: *they* shall not get through!"[10]

And they do not get through. But it was too late to stop them from entering Dixmude. Their musketry was all round us, a rifle behind every heap of rubble, a machine-gun at every point of vantage. The sharp note of the German trumpet sounded from every side. It is possible that a certain number of the enemy who had lain hidden in the cellars of Dixmude ever since the fighting on the 25th now came out of their earth to add to the confusion. The truth of this will be known some day. We were under fire in the town, outside the town, on the canal, on the Yser. It was street fighting, with all its ambuscades and surprises. What had become of the covering troops in the cemetery and on the Beerst road? Of the reserve under Commander Rabot, driven from ditch to ditch, its commander killed or missing,[11] only fifteen men were left. These were rallied by Lieutenant Sérieyx in a muddy ditch, where they fought to the last man. Surrounded and disarmed, Sérieyx and some others were forced to act as a shield to the Germans who were advancing against the junction of the canal and the Yser. "Abominable sight,"

repulsed. He supported his sufferings without complaint, and in the evening, although he was very weak, they moved him on to Malo-les-Bains, for he "wished to die on French ground."

10. Dr. Caradec, *op. cit.*

11. He was killed. He had been hit by a bullet above the ear as he raised himself to glance round over the high bank of a watercourse lined by his men.

says Lieutenant A., "French prisoners compelled to march in front of Boches, who knelt behind them and fired between their legs!" Our men beyond the Yser could not reply.

"Call to them to surrender," ordered the German major to Sérieyx.

"Why should you think they will surrender? There are ten thousand of them!"[12] There were really two hundred!

At this moment a sudden burst of fire on the right distracted the enemy's attention. With a sign to the others, Sérieyx, whose arm had already been broken by a bullet, threw himself into the Yser, succeeded in swimming across, and at once made his way to the admiral to report what was happening.

A counter-attack ordered by the officer in command of the defence and led by Lieutenant d'Albia had covered his escape. The eighth company, in reserve, reinforced by a section of the fifth company of the 2nd Regiment, under Commander Mauros and Lieutenant Daniel, entrenched itself behind the barricade at the level crossing on the Eessen road.[13] On all the roads leading to the Yser, and especially at the three bridges, sections strongly established themselves or helped to consolidate sections already there. Would these dispositions, hastily taken by Commandant Delage, be enough to save Dixmude? At most they could only prolong the agony. Her hours were numbered. After having driven its way through the hostile column which had reached the Yser, Lieutenant d'Albia's section encountered more Germans debouching from the Grand' Place and neighbouring streets. Germans and Frenchmen now formed nothing but a mass of shouting men. They shot

---

12. To this major Sérieyx had only surrendered after all his ammunition was exhausted, and he and his men saw that no further resistance was possible. The major had then asked Sérieyx whether there was no means of crossing the Yser. Sérieyx answered, "I only know of one, the Haut Pont." Now, at some fifty yards from where they stood, there was a footbridge which our sailors were at that moment crossing. Sérieyx held the major's attention by taking a pencil and tracing a complicated plan of the position. From time to time firing took place, and the Frenchmen planted themselves stoically in front of the Boches, Sérieyx working away at his plan. But the major grew impatient at its complication, and thought it better to make use of his prisoner to procure the surrender of the trenches.

13. "The troops in the southern sector moved back towards the town, defending themselves by a series of barricades, under the orders of Commander Mauros and Lieutenant Daniel." (Note-book of Second-Lieutenant X.)

each other at close quarters; they fought with their bayonets, their knives, their clubbed rifles, and when these were broken, with their fists, with their feet, even with their teeth. By three in the afternoon we had lost one half of our men, killed, wounded, or prisoners. The German columns were still pouring into Dixmude through the breaches in the defence. They pushed us back to the bridges, which we still held, which we were indeed to hold to the end. They were going to take Dixmude, but the little sailor was right: they were not going to pass the Yser. One more attack was organised to bring off the Mauros company, which was retiring under a terrible fire. The remains of several sections were brought together, and, led by their officers, they charged into the *mêlée* in the streets. One purple-faced, sweating marine, who had seen his brother fall, swore he would have the blood of twenty Boches. He went for them with the bayonet, counting "One! two! three!" etc., till he had reached twenty-two. After that he returned to his company, a madman.

But what could the finest heroism do against the swarms of men who rose, as it were, from the earth as fast as they were crushed? "They are like bugs," sighed a quartermaster, and night was coming on. Dixmude had ceased to give signs of life. For six hours fighting had gone on over a dismembered corpse. Not a gable, not a wall, was left standing, except those of the flour factory. To hold these heaps of rubbish, which might turn into a focus of infection, was not worth the little finger of one of our men. At 5 o'clock in the evening, after blowing up the bridges and the flour factory, the admiral retired behind the Yser.[14]

---

14. It has been said that an old woman caused the fall of Dixmude on November 10. "The allied forces occupying Dixmude," said the *Daily Mail*, "consisted of a squadron of cavalry encamped on the right bank of the Yser, two batteries of 75s, a regiment of infantry, and a battalion of Zouaves (!). The battle began with a violent cannonade, which had the great distillery in the centre of the town as its principal objective. Two of our 75s were on the first floor of a tannery, the others below, on a little mound where skins were cleaned. Our artillery was able to hold the enemy in check, opening great breaches through the hostile ranks with its shells. One German gun lost all its team, and the Uhlans were mown down by our sailors. Our men, cavalry and infantry, were awaiting the word to attack. Just at this moment appeared an old woman to whom our Zouaves had been kind, as she seemed so miserable. She had marched with them, leaning on the arm of one and another and sharing their soup. She mounted to the first floor of the tannery, and then disappeared. A moment later a light appeared on the roof of the distillery. (continued on next page)

110

A marine wrote a few days later from Audierne:

Dear mother,
I have to tell you that on the 10th of this month I was not cheering much at Dixmude, for out of the whole of my company only 30 returned. I never expected to come out, but with a stout heart I managed to get away. I had a very bad time. Many of us had to swim to save ourselves.

These, no doubt, were the prisoners who had thrown themselves into the canal with the heroic Sérieyx.

All this time Lieutenant Cantener, who had taken command on the death of his senior officer, had been maintaining himself on the Beerst road, with three companies of marines. At nightfall he had the satisfaction—and the credit—of bringing nearly the whole of his command safely into our lines. They had made their way by ditches full of water and mud up to their waists. They were 450 in all—450 blocks of mud—and they were not, as has been said, worn out and without arms and equipment, but steadily marching in fours, bayonets fixed, and as calm as on parade. They had their wounded in front, and each company had its rear-guard.[15]

It was seen to swing three times from right to left. Five minutes later the German shells began to rain upon the point indicated by the light. In a very short time the building was greatly damaged, fires broke out, and the burning alcohol lighted up the whole neighbourhood. Unable to stem either the deluge of shells or this conflagration, the French general decided to evacuate the town and entrench himself on the canal banks. With great difficulty the 75s were withdrawn from their positions. Before quitting the city the French soldiers saw, and were able to identify, the 'old woman,' stretched on the ground, with the uniform of an Uhlan peeping from beneath 'her' skirts." This is all pure imagination. Spies certainly played a part in the fall of Dixmude. Too many people were accepted as refugees and distressed inhabitants who were in reality the guides and accomplices of the enemy. But, in the first place, we had no Zouaves at Dixmude; secondly, our observation post was not in a tannery; finally, we had no cavalry. The only body which barred the way to the Germans was the marines, omitted in this account.

15. The following details of this fine operation have reached me, but before giving them I must remind the reader that the Germans who fell upon the reserve under Commander Rabot did not destroy Company 11. This company, after a lively exchange of fire, retired upon Companies 9 and 10, which were almost intact. Dixmude had already fallen, when the captains of the three companies met, and after thinking over the situation, determined to hold on at all costs. Consequently "Company 10 proceeded to place a small advanced post on the Beerst road, with two double sentries, and a rear-guard at the old mill. (continued on next page)

Too many of our men were left beneath the ruins of the town or in the hands of the enemy, but they had not been vainly sacrificed.[16] After losing some 10,000 men,[17] the Germans found themselves in possession of a town reduced to mere heaps of rubbish with an impregnable line beyond. Our reserve lines had become our front, well furnished with heavy guns, and punctually supported by the inundation which stretched its impassable defence both to north and south. The whole valley of the Lower Yser had become a tide-less sea, out into which stood Dixmude, like a crumbling headland. In taking it the Germans had simply made themselves masters of

---

The company itself was drawn up with one rank facing to the front, the other to the rear, and the trenches so arranged that a front could be shown in any direction. The machine-guns abandoned by the Belgians were overhauled and placed so as to sweep the Beerst road. At 6.30 the little northern post was attacked. Pursuant to orders, it retired after a volley or two. Then fire opened along the whole line, the machine-guns of Company 10 joining in. The Germans, who expected no such stubborn resistance, had severe losses. For an hour the fight lasted without change, the men still at their post and the trench still intact. All the killed, Captain Baudry among them, were shot through the head, the wounded, in the head or the arm, in the act of firing. At this moment the beginning of an attack from the rear made itself felt. The time for retreat had come, as the detachment had lost connection with the staff of the battalion. The companies moved off successively, each leaving a section to protect its retreat. This retreat was admirable, but quite indescribable on account of the ground. *Arroyos* (mud-holes) everywhere. The men got through, although sinking to their armpits and handing on their wounded before them. After two hours of this painful but orderly progression, they arrived before the footbridge over the Yser. A farm granary arose near by, where the Germans had mounted machine-guns to sweep the bridge. Lieutenant Cantener, who was now in command, decided to carry the farm. The operation was a complete success. The Germans were driven out, the farm burnt, and the Yser crossed. The column, with its wounded in front, then made its way safely to the cross-roads at Caeskerke, and thence into the shelter trenches at Oudecappelle." The third battalion of the 1st Regiment, which held the northern sector, had the following officers: Company 9, Berat, Poisson, Le Gall; Company 10, Baudry, Mazen, Devisse; Company 11, Cantener, Hillairet, Le Provost; Company 12, De Nanteuil, Vielhomme, Charrier.

16. According to M. Pierre Loti, the marines at Dixmude lost "half their effective and from 80 to 100 of their officers." This estimate is none too large if we include the wounded and missing.

17. According to the *Nieuws van den Dag*, 4,000 wounded were sent to Liège the next day. Another Dutch journal, the *Telegraaf*, says that out of 3,000 men engaged in the attack on the southern sector of the defence "only a hundred men were left after the fall of the town." All estimates are clearly uncertain in such confused affairs, and so we have taken our figures preferably from the neutral press, in which we may look for a certain amount of impartiality.

THE INUNDATION—OLD MILL AND FARMS ON THE YSER

two *têtes de pont*. Even that is saying too much, for we still commanded the place from the northern bank of the Yser, and our artillery, under General Coffec, frustrated all attempts to organise their capture. Meanwhile thousands of Germans, between the Yser and the embankment of the Nieuport railway, watched with apprehension the water rising about the mounds up which they had hauled their mortars and machine-guns. In the immediate neighbourhood of Dixmude, where the admiral had caused the sluice at the sixteenth milestone to be blown up,[18] a hostile column of some fifteen hundred men was overwhelmed by the water together with the patch of raised ground on which it had taken refuge.[19] A fresh inundation added greatly to the extent of the floods, and practically reconstituted the old *schoore* of Dixmude. All danger of the enemy's making good the passage of the river had finally passed away.

---

18. The operation was carried out by Quartermaster Le Bellé to whom the military medal was awarded. "A night or two ago," writes Commander Geynet, "I was ordered to blow up the sluice in front of me.... A little quartermaster crossed the stream on a plank nailed across two barrels. We pushed the Prussians out of the way by rifle fire. My little man, with his charge of dynamite, chose his moment well, then, leaving his raft to draw the fire of the Prussians, regained our bank by swimming."
19. Paul Chautard in the *Liberté* of November 24. Commander Geynet says nothing of this episode, however.

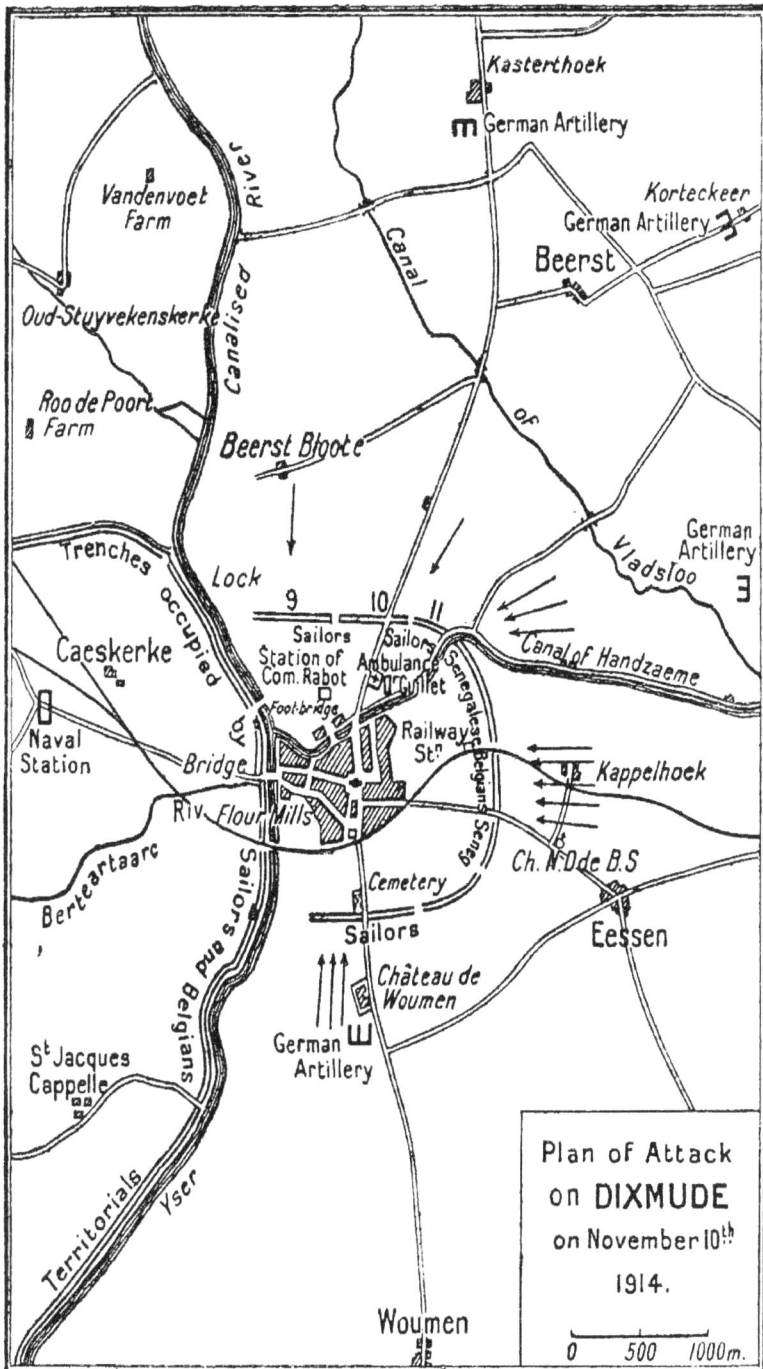

Kasterhoek

m German Artillery

Vandenvoet Farm

River

Canalised

Canal

Korteckeer

German Artillery

Beerst

Oud-Stuyvekenskerke

Roo de Poort Farm

Beerst Bloote

of

German Artillery

Vladsloo

Trenches occupied

Lock

9   10   11

Caeskerke

Sailors Station of Com. Rabot

Sailors Ambulance N° Gullet

Canal of Handzaeme

Senegalese

Belgians

Sens

Foot-bridge

Railway St°

Naval Station

Bridge

Riv. Flour Mills

Kappelhoek

Berteartaarc

Sailors and Belgians

Cemetery

Sailors

Ch. N°D de B.S

Eessen

St Jacques Cappelle

Château de Woumen

German Artillery

Territorials

Yser

Plan of Attack
on **DIXMUDE**
on November 10th
1914.

0   500   1000 m.

Woumen

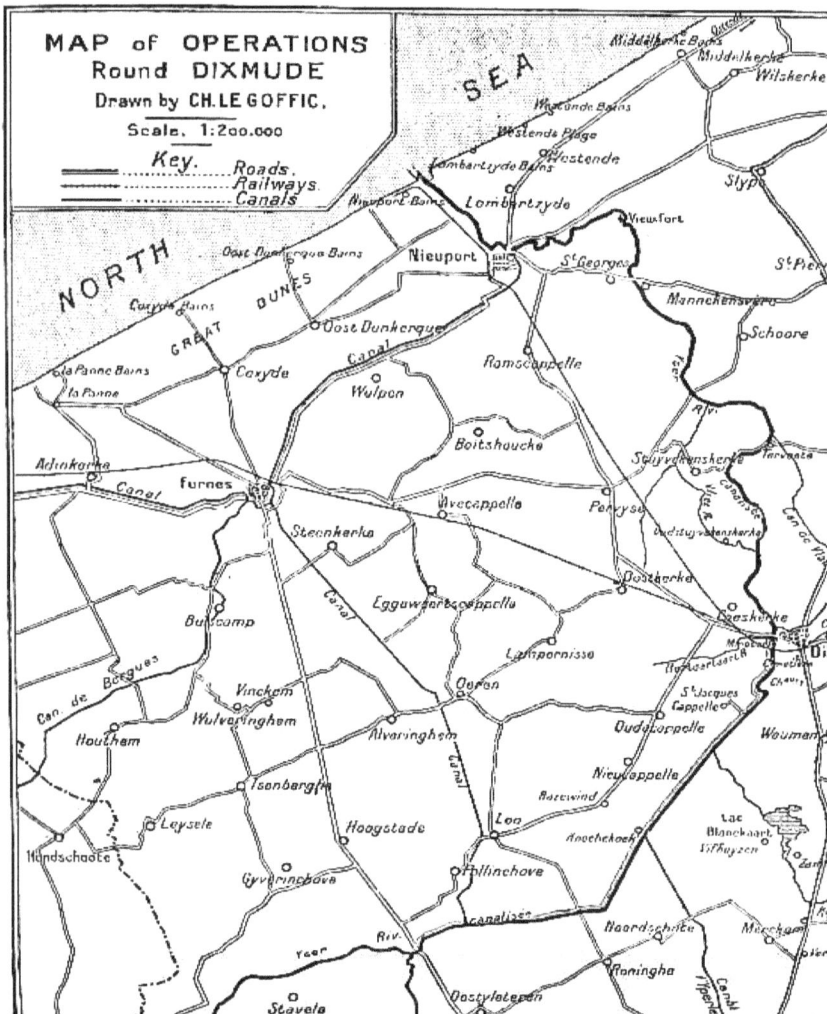

MAP of OPERATIONS
Round DIXMUDE

Drawn by CH. LE GOFFIC.

Scale, 1:200,000

Key.
———————— Roads.
·························· Railways.
— — — — — Canals

SEA

NORTH

Middelkerke Bains · Middelkerke · Wilskerke

Westende Bains · Westende Plage · Westende

Lombartzyde Bains · Lombartzyde · Slype

Nieuport Bains · Nieuwfort

Oost Dunkerque Bains · Nieuport · St Georges · St Pier

Coxyde Bains · GREAT DUNES · Mannekensvere · Schoore

la Panne Bains · la Panne · Coxyde · Oost Dunkerque · Canal · Ramscappelle · Riv.

Wulpen · Boitshoucke · Schyvekenskerke · Tervaete

Adinkerke · Canal · Furnes · Avecappelle · Pervyse · Oudstuyvekenskerke · Can de Yse

Steenkerke · Canal · Eggewaertscappelle · Oostkerke · Vis &

Buscamp · Lampernisse · Caeskerke · Di

Can. de Bergues · Vinckem · Wulveringhem · Ooren · St Jacques Cappelle · Oudecappelle · Weuman · Chuys · Het Aderlandt

Houthem · Isenbarghe · Alveringhem · Canal · Nieucappelle · Reninge

Leysele · Hoogstade · Loo · Beerwind · Anschekaek · Lac Blanckaart · Sifhuyzen · Zar

Hondschoote · Gyverinchove · Pillinchove · Noordschitte · Merckem · Bler

Yser · Riv. · Canalisée · Reninghe · Can. Ypre

Stavele · Oostvleteren · Bixsch

Battle & Retreat of Melle.

Eecloo · Erterude · Wachtebeke · Clusyen · Saffelaere · Somergem · Evergem · Oostacker · Boesi

Knesselaere · Oorwinthel · Sleydinge · Ronsel

St Georges · Aalsel · Lovendegem

Bellem · Hamme · Meerendré · Mariakerke · Adelgem · Loochristy · Mayere · Oudenhout

Aeltre · Biesemvelde · Hansbeke · Loaveld · Luchteren · GHENT · Gentbrugge · Laerne · Breton

Wiggene · Ruysselede · Lootenhule · Paesele · Nevele · Afsne · Gh · Ledeberg · Melle · Wessegem · Quatrecht

Rille · Schuy · Peruxcappelle · Canegnem · Wyncke · Yousden · Moortzeele · Oudrech

Eeghem · THIELT · Zeveren · De Pinte · Morelbeke · Dombegge · Bontroch · Cyronale

Attem · Wontergem · Burnia · Asten · Seuerghem · Oudenaeter · Braystraet

Moorseele · Oontergem · Greffmene · Nauwceth · Leck · Machelen · Makeire · Ronsberg

LEONAUR

ALSO FROM LEONAUR
AVAILABLE IN SOFTCOVER OR HARDCOVER WITH DUST JACKET

THE FALL OF THE MOGHUL EMPIRE OF HINDUSTAN *by H. G. Keene*—
By the beginning of the nineteenth century, as British and Indian armies under Lake
and Wellesley dominated the scene, a little over half a century of conflict brought the
Moghul Empire to its knees.

LADY SALE'S AFGHANISTAN *by Florentia Sale*—An Indomitable Victorian
Lady's Account of the Retreat from Kabul During the First Afghan War.

THE CAMPAIGN OF MAGENTA AND SOLFERINO 1859 *by Harold Car-
michael Wylly*—The Decisive Conflict for the Unification of Italy.

FRENCH'S CAVALRY CAMPAIGN *by J. G. Maydon*—A Special Correspo-
nent's View of British Army Mounted Troops During the Boer War.

CAVALRY AT WATERLOO *by Sir Evelyn Wood*—British Mounted Troops
During the Campaign of 1815.

THE SUBALTERN *by George Robert Gleig*—The Experiences of an Officer of
the 85th Light Infantry During the Peninsular War.

NAPOLEON AT BAY, 1814 *by F. Loraine Petre*—The Campaigns to the Fall of
the First Empire.

NAPOLEON AND THE CAMPAIGN OF 1806 *by Colonel Vachée*—The Napoleonic Method of Organisation and Command to the Battles of Jena & Auerstädt.

THE COMPLETE ADVENTURES IN THE CONNAUGHT RANGERS *by
William Grattan*—The 88th Regiment during the Napoleonic Wars by a Serving
Officer.

BUGLER AND OFFICER OF THE RIFLES *by William Green & Harry
Smith*—With the 95th (Rifles) during the Peninsular & Waterloo Campaigns of the
Napoleonic Wars.

NAPOLEONIC WAR STORIES *by Sir Arthur Quiller-Couch*—Tales of soldiers,
spies, battles & sieges from the Peninsular & Waterloo campaingns.

CAPTAIN OF THE 95TH (RIFLES) *by Jonathan Leach*—An officer of Wel-
lington's sharpshooters during the Peninsular, South of France and Waterloo campaigns of the Napoleonic wars.

RIFLEMAN COSTELLO *by Edward Costello*—The adventures of a soldier of
the 95th (Rifles) in the Peninsular & Waterloo Campaigns of the Napoleonic wars.

LEONAUR

ALSO FROM LEONAUR
AVAILABLE IN SOFTCOVER OR HARDCOVER WITH DUST JACKET

ZULU:1879 *by D.C.F. Moodie & the Leonaur Editors*—The Anglo-Zulu War of 1879 from contemporary sources: First Hand Accounts, Interviews, Dispatches, Official Documents & Newspaper Reports.

THE RED DRAGOON *by W.J. Adams*—With the 7th Dragoon Guards in the Cape of Good Hope against the Boers & the Kaffir tribes during the 'war of the axe' 1843-48'.

THE RECOLLECTIONS OF SKINNER OF SKINNER'S HORSE *by James Skinner*—James Skinner and his 'Yellow Boys' Irregular cavalry in the wars of India between the British, Mahratta, Rajput, Mogul, Sikh & Pindarree Forces.

A CAVALRY OFFICER DURING THE SEPOY REVOLT *by A. R. D. Mackenzie*—Experiences with the 3rd Bengal Light Cavalry, the Guides and Sikh Irregular Cavalry from the outbreak to Delhi and Lucknow.

A NORFOLK SOLDIER IN THE FIRST SIKH WAR *by J W Baldwin*—Experiences of a private of H.M. 9th Regiment of Foot in the battles for the Punjab, India 1845-6.

TOMMY ATKINS' WAR STORIES: 14 FIRST HAND ACCOUNTS—Fourteen first hand accounts from the ranks of the British Army during Queen Victoria's Empire.

THE WATERLOO LETTERS *by H. T. Siborne*—Accounts of the Battle by British Officers for its Foremost Historian.

NEY: GENERAL OF CAVALRY VOLUME 1—1769-1799 *by Antoine Bulos*—The Early Career of a Marshal of the First Empire.

NEY: MARSHAL OF FRANCE VOLUME 2—1799-1805 *by Antoine Bulos*—The Early Career of a Marshal of the First Empire.

AIDE-DE-CAMP TO NAPOLEON *by Philippe-Paul de Ségur*—For anyone interested in the Napoleonic Wars this book, written by one who was intimate with the strategies and machinations of the Emperor, will be essential reading.

TWILIGHT OF EMPIRE *by Sir Thomas Ussher & Sir George Cockburn*—Two accounts of Napoleon's Journeys in Exile to Elba and St. Helena: Narrative of Events by Sir Thomas Ussher & Napoleon's Last Voyage: Extract of a diary by Sir George Cockburn.

PRIVATE WHEELER *by William Wheeler*—The letters of a soldier of the 51st Light Infantry during the Peninsular War & at Waterloo.

LEONAUR

ALSO FROM LEONAUR
AVAILABLE IN SOFTCOVER OR HARDCOVER WITH DUST JACKET

BUGEAUD: A PACK WITH A BATON *by Thomas Robert Bugeaud*—The Early Campaigns of a Soldier of Napoleon's Army Who Would Become a Marshal of France.

WATERLOO RECOLLECTIONS *by Frederick Llewellyn*—Rare First Hand Accounts, Letters, Reports and Retellings from the Campaign of 1815.

SERGEANT NICOL *by Daniel Nicol*—The Experiences of a Gordon Highlander During the Napoleonic Wars in Egypt, the Peninsula and France.

THE JENA CAMPAIGN: 1806 *by F. N. Maude*—The Twin Battles of Jena & Auerstadt Between Napoleon's French and the Prussian Army.

PRIVATE O'NEIL *by Charles O'Neil*—The recollections of an Irish Rogue of H. M. 28th Regt.—The Slashers—during the Peninsula & Waterloo campaigns of the Napoleonic war.

ROYAL HIGHLANDER *by James Anton*—A soldier of H.M 42nd (Royal) Highlanders during the Peninsular, South of France & Waterloo Campaigns of the Napoleonic Wars.

CAPTAIN BLAZE *by Elzéar Blaze*—Life in Napoleons Army.

LEJEUNE VOLUME 1 *by Louis-François Lejeune*—The Napoleonic Wars through the Experiences of an Officer on Berthier's Staff.

LEJEUNE VOLUME 2 *by Louis-François Lejeune*—The Napoleonic Wars through the Experiences of an Officer on Berthier's Staff.

CAPTAIN COIGNET *by Jean-Roch Coignet*—A Soldier of Napoleon's Imperial Guard from the Italian Campaign to Russia and Waterloo.

FUSILIER COOPER *by John S. Cooper*—Experiences in the 7th (Royal) Fusiliers During the Peninsular Campaign of the Napoleonic Wars and the American Campaign to New Orleans.

FIGHTING NAPOLEON'S EMPIRE *by Joseph Anderson*—The Campaigns of a British Infantryman in Italy, Egypt, the Peninsular & the West Indies During the Napoleonic Wars.

CHASSEUR BARRES *by Jean-Baptiste Barres*—The experiences of a French Infantryman of the Imperial Guard at Austerlitz, Jena, Eylau, Friedland, in the Peninsular, Lutzen, Bautzen, Zinnwald and Hanau during the Napoleonic Wars.

LEONAUR

ALSO FROM LEONAUR
AVAILABLE IN SOFTCOVER OR HARDCOVER WITH DUST JACKET

FARAWAY CAMPAIGN *by F. James*—Experiences of an Indian Army Cavalry Officer in Persia & Russia During the Great War.

REVOLT IN THE DESERT *by T. E. Lawrence*—An account of the experiences of one remarkable British officer's war from his own perspective.

MACHINE-GUN SQUADRON *by A. M. G.*—The 20th Machine Gunners from British Yeomanry Regiments in the Middle East Campaign of the First World War.

A GUNNER'S CRUSADE *by Antony Bluett*—The Campaign in the Desert, Palestine & Syria as Experienced by the Honourable Artillery Company During the Great War .

DESPATCH RIDER *by W. H. L. Watson*—The Experiences of a British Army Motorcycle Despatch Rider During the Opening Battles of the Great War in Europe.

TIGERS ALONG THE TIGRIS *by E. J. Thompson*—The Leicestershire Regiment in Mesopotamia During the First World War.

HEARTS & DRAGONS *by Charles R. M. F. Crutwell*—The 4th Royal Berkshire Regiment in France and Italy During the Great War, 1914-1918.

INFANTRY BRIGADE: 1914 *by John Ward*—The Diary of a Commander of the 15th Infantry Brigade, 5th Division, British Army, During the Retreat from Mons.

DOING OUR 'BIT' *by Ian Hay*—Two Classic Accounts of the Men of Kitchener's 'New Army' During the Great War including *The First 100,000* & *All In It*.

AN EYE IN THE STORM *by Arthur Ruhl*—An American War Correspondent's Experiences of the First World War from the Western Front to Gallipoli-and Beyond.

STAND & FALL *by Joe Cassells*—With the Middlesex Regiment Against the Bolsheviks 1918-19.

RIFLEMAN MACGILL'S WAR *by Patrick MacGill*—A Soldier of the London Irish During the Great War in Europe including *The Amateur Army*, *The Red Horizon* & *The Great Push*.

WITH THE GUNS *by C. A. Rose & Hugh Dalton*—Two First Hand Accounts of British Gunners at War in Europe During World War 1- Three Years in France with the Guns and With the British Guns in Italy.

THE BUSH WAR DOCTOR *by Robert V. Dolbey*—The Experiences of a British Army Doctor During the East African Campaign of the First World War.

www.ingramcontent.com/pod-product-compliance
Lightning Source LLC
Chambersburg PA
CBHW031854090426
42741CB00005B/495